# IMMIGRANTS' JOURNEYS:

## Africans Making Canada Home

CHIFUKA M CHUNDU

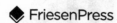
FriesenPress

One Printers Way
Altona, MB
R0G0B0
Canada

www.friesenpress.com

ISBN
978-1-03-911845-4 (Hardcover)
978-1-03-911844-7 (Paperback)
978-1-03-911846-1 (eBook)

*Social Science, Emigration & Immigration*

Distributed to the trade by The Ingram Book Company

# TABLE OF CONTENTS

# INTRODUCTION

I n the following pages, you will journey with individuals who migrated to or grew up in Canada between their childhood and young adult years.

**A word of caution is recommended for younger readers who may not be able to fully process some of the sensitive nature of the subjects covered and the traumatic experiences retold here.**

The stories aim to educate and help normalize conversations on issues that often go undiscussed in immigrant circles, as well as to open a window into the lives of immigrants to Canada. The stories are taken from individuals who have dealt with post-traumatic stress disorder, anxiety, sexual and physical abuse, loneliness, and divorce, among other challenges.

Perhaps you are just curious about the lives of Canadian immigrants and the challenges they experience in Canada. Maybe you are a parent who has brought your family to Canada to experience a better life. You may be a couple suddenly faced with conflict that never existed in your marriage before you migrated. Or you might be a young person trying to figure out why you and your parents never seem to see eye to eye on anything. You might be on a journey, trying to find your place in Canadian society now that you suddenly find yourself being labelled "a minority."

As you read the pages of this book, you will find people who have been in similar situations and have walked the same road you might be travelling. The stories range from humorous to sad, from tragic to inspiring, and some of the experiences retold in this book will likely resonate with you.

The stories in this book are one hundred per cent true but for the fact that the real names and ages of the individuals have been changed to protect their identities. Interviews with various experts in the fields of psychology, psychiatry, medicine, and family therapy have been included at the end of each section to address some common issues in the stories shared.

I hope that by reading this book you will be inspired to be a better version of yourself, to keep believing that dreams can come true, to keep hoping there can be a better tomorrow, and to keep faith that there is more to life than the situation you may find yourself in right now.

# Part 1:
# The Immigration
# Experience in Childhood

I t is often assumed that individuals that migrate as children are resilient to change and do not deal with as much adjustment to the new country as their parents do. However, children can go through as much if not more stress than most adults assume. Falling grades, loss of confidence, withdrawal, aggressive or rebellious behaviours can be some signs pointing to the fact that a child might be having a hard time coping with the sudden changes taking place around them.

As a parent, it can be quite concerning to see sudden changes in your children. Your son has started wearing his pants at knee level and recently pierced his ears. You just found out that your daughter has been dating someone secretly, her dressing choices are not ones you approve of, her accent has changed, and she won't speak her mother tongue anymore. You look at your friends that have lived in Canada longer than you have and you see their kids marrying people of different races and forsaking their parents' religion. The house is constantly filled with tension and stress. Everyone seems to be speaking a different language and you are at a loss to know how to respond appropriately. You wonder to yourself how to deal with all of it. Did you make a mistake in choosing to come to Canada?

Perhaps you are a young person in your parent's home and counting down the days until you turn eighteen so you can leave and escape their control. Things have gone down so bad with them you feel there is no use in trying anymore.

If you can relate to these experiences, you are not alone. Moving to a new country can be traumatic, and children even as young as four or five go through enormous amounts of stress because of the migration process. If the trauma of the process is not dealt with correctly, it carries right into young adulthood and adulthood, and eventually manifests itself in one form or the other as the stories in Part 1 will demonstrate.

# Chapter 1:
# Being Unique is Okay
By J. A., 26-year-old female

I am originally from Zimbabwe. I was born in the nineties, and I'm the first of four children. My parents have always been nomads with a sense of adventure. Around the year 2002, my family and I moved to the United Kingdom, and it was there that I started primary school. After spending four years in the UK, my parents decided to move back to Zimbabwe. Within a year of our return to Zimbabwe, we left for South Africa, where I finished the rest of my primary school. In 2008, Dad left for Canada, and me, my two sisters, and brother moved back to Zimbabwe with our mother. We stayed in Zimbabwe for three years before we joined Dad in Canada in 2011.

## STRUGGLES WITH MY IDENTITY

Up to this point, I had moved around a lot, so I was used to the experience of settling in new countries. But when we got to Canada, I found it very challenging trying to fit in. With all our moves before, I was younger and was not as aware of what was happening, but this time I was cognizant of the

> *With all our moves before, I was younger and was not as aware of what was happening, but this time I was cognizant of the changes taking place.*

changes taking place. I wanted to fit in, make friends, and live a normal life. I had just turned thirteen and I remember being very self-conscious. I remember feeling, *It's different here.* The people dressed differently and they thought differently. By the time I was about seventeen, I started to ask myself, *How much do I really want to fit in? How much of myself is still Zimbabwean?* I started to question how much I knew about my people. I wanted to learn more about my culture and where I came from. I had lost my mother tongue and could only speak English. At home in the UK, we spoke only English right until we came to Canada. I spoke Shona as a toddler, but my parents, through no fault of their own and through exposure to travelling, made me lose my mother tongue.

It was about the same time when even my parents seemed to come to the realization that they had not taught us enough about their culture. Dad now wanted all of us to visit Zimbabwe because he was afraid that we were losing our roots. My parents started to speak a bit of Shona in the house, and we started to listen to more Shona music just to remind ourselves a bit of our culture. It was a time in my life where I was freaking out and my parents were freaking out. It was almost as if we were all having midlife crises.

I started writing poetry and that helped me start my enquiry into my roots. I really struggled with my identity. I was growing stronger in my Christian faith in my late teens. As a child of God, I saw myself as a citizen of the world but I considered myself Zimbabwean. I also got my Canadian citizenship around that time. So while I was now Canadian, I still identified more closely with my Zimbabwean/African roots, and that's the posture I have chosen to maintain because I realized that fitting in isn't my goal. Being comfortable with being unique regarding where I come from and who I am is what I aim for. Previously, I would have said the place where I am is what I identify with. But who's to say what I am? Who's to say I am Black enough or Zimbabwean enough?

I studied to learn how to speak Shona, but even when I go back home sometimes, I get the whole "You are different" talk when I am there. The truth is, I have always been different. When I am in my homeland, I am different. When I am in Canada I am different. So, I have decided that being unique is okay. Embrace all that you are. I embrace the fact that I am Zimbabwean and that I am Black, and that I am Canadian.

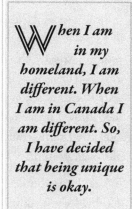

*When I am in my homeland, I am different. When I am in Canada I am different. So, I have decided that being unique is okay.*

## ME AND MY PARENTS

The time between the ages of sixteen and eighteen was hard for me, as it is for everyone those ages. My relationship with my parents was great before that, but we struggled in my late teens. Before coming to Canada, there were a lot of years when I didn't live with my father, so finally being together with him was awesome. I got to know him again. I had always lived with my mom and my relationship with her was better. In my later teen years, I was trying to discover myself without my family but while in my parents' home. I was always a quiet and respectful child, but I also struggled with things of my own.

When I was fifteen, I started to get spasms. I was diagnosed with a generalized anxiety disorder, but at the time I didn't know what the spasms were. My mom had taken me to the doctor and I got some pills but I never really followed through with taking them, even though I knew something was wrong with me. I only got the proper diagnosis two years after starting the medication. I was going through a lot of mental pressure, but in an African household such things are stigmatized. If I said, "I'm struggling with things in my mind," my parents would just say, "You need to pray more; come to Jesus." I was really struggling and that significantly impacted my relationship with my parents. I felt they were not listening to me. I also know I hurt them; there was hurt on both sides. We had our good times, but there was always that hurt lingering in the background.

When I was about eighteen, there was conflict all around my family. I was making decisions about university and my own financial freedom and decided to get a job as a nanny. My relationship with my mom was going down the drain, my parents' marriage was having its struggles, and I felt that we were all just growing apart. My relationship with my dad suffered. He struggles with seasonal affective disorder, so he would be someone else, depending on the weather. Our relationship went downhill. We stopped talking. It was bad.

We would have long prayer nights in our home—my parents mostly talked and lectured. But the older I got, the more I'd start to speak up, so dialogue started to open bit by bit. But it was me as the older child who initiated dialogue. I wanted a change and it had to come from me. I eventually moved out of my parents' house and that was my way of saying, "I can't do this anymore." My mental health was suffering. I wasn't strong; I was really weak, so I moved out. That caused a lot of pain for my parents. But after a couple of months, I explained what I was feeling at the time, and we had that hard discussion. They talked about the things they went through when I left, but I just decided that my actions needed to speak for themselves. I'd go and visit every weekend, and I'd talk to them about what was happening in my mind with my mental health. I'd tell them about my visits to the doctors.

## THE GENERATIONAL DIVIDE

I feel like people of my generation believe parents need to talk and to get to know their kids. In Africa, we have the village concept where children talk about issues with relatives and other people in the community. Since we don't have that here in Canada, African children hurt badly in this society. My parents grew up with the whole, "You only speak when you are spoken to" mentality, so bringing up issues to them was quite challenging and things burst out badly when they

My parents grew up with the whole, "You only speak when you are spoken to" mentality, so bringing up issues to them was quite challenging finally come out. I had an outburst at my parents one time and even I was surprised at the things I said. That caused a big rift between us, but we never talked about it afterwards. My sister was also going through mental challenges of her own, so my parents got to see it through her eyes and started to believe that our mental health challenges were a real thing. They still don't fully get it, but it's better. A lot of people in our family go through mental health challenges, but we don't talk about it. It's important to talk about things and it is just as important to protect your peace as well. Sometimes I say to myself, *There is this issue right now, but if I tackle it with the way I'm feeling, it's not going to go well.* So I take a few days or even a few weeks before I talk about it. In the end, I believe a relationship may not become perfect, but even for just a bit of improvement, it's worth the fight to make things better.

# Chapter 2:
# Suffering in Silence
By J. O., 22-year-old female

I am 22 years old. I immigrated to Canada from West Africa with my family when I was seven months old. I grew up around a lot of African norms: the culture, food, and language.

## LIVING AS A 1.5-GENERATION IMMIGRANT

Navigating my culture as an African and as a Canadian has been a struggle at times. There are some things my parents talk about that are not an issue for me, and there are some things that I'll talk about that my parents are unable to understand. But just because you can't see something as an issue doesn't mean that it isn't an issue or struggle for that other person. Being the child of an immigrant and being a 1.5-generation immigrant (immigrants who are born in their home countries but technically are from their adopted home because they were raised in their adopted home) is challenging in and of itself. Adjusting to the new culture while maintaining the culture of your homeland is something no amount of education, well- adjusted mentality, or perseverance can prepare you for.

9

> *Adjusting to the new culture while maintaining the culture of your homeland is something no amount of education, well-adjusted mentality, or perseverance can prepare you for.*

I think many parents try to do the best they can, but sometimes that creates awkward situations for the kids. For example, a new immigrant child may end up being teased at school for what she is wearing or the food she brings for lunch. Not that what I ate or wore was bad—it was amazing. But my parents wouldn't understand if I complained to them and told them what was happening at school because sometimes they just didn't know any better. I remember being seven or eight years old and being made fun of for my name, not because it was hard to pronounce but because it was different. It's hard being different when you are a kid. Now I look at myself and say, "I found that difficult at that time" even though those were not such big issues.

It's a challenge for parents to know how to successfully integrate their children without having them experience bullying or teasing. I think it's important for parents to teach their kids to be proud of their differences and hold on to their identity, especially because they are in a different country. For me, my parents may have missed the fact that even though they wanted me to hold on to my culture, sometimes it just hurt because I was made fun of. It was difficult for my parents to adjust and find work but it was also hard for me as a kid even though I was being raised here.

People assume immigrant kids should have an easy time settling in, but it can be very difficult. I spoke English, but I was home a lot. I didn't go to daycare, so I spoke my native language most of the time. Because of that, I spoke English with an accent. I was raised in Canada, but it was almost as if I was living in this African bubble within Canada.

> People assume immigrant kids should have an easy time settling in, but it can be very difficult.

Your primary community is your parents or guardians, and if you feel like you can't relate well to them it makes whatever issue you are going through that much harder, especially if the issue is coming from them. When I was young, my parents wouldn't allow me to go to sleepovers. I'm older now and understand why they didn't, but all my other friends from other ethnic backgrounds were allowed to go to sleepovers, and that was very difficult for me. Things like that tend to drive a wedge in the parent–child relationship when parents don't bother to explain things in a way that makes sense to the child. Eventually, the child talks to the parent about some things but avoids talking to them about other things.

## THINKING ABOUT MENTAL HEALTH

I have had challenges with my mental health. I feel it was a few events that set things off, but as I have walked my mental health journey, I think I have a predisposition to some of the things I struggle with. I can remember being very young, maybe about six to eight, and thinking about suicide and being fixated on it like it was a normal thing. Some traumatic events had happened prior, but those things didn't really bother me. I felt it was normal to have such thoughts at such a

11

young age. It was normal for me to imagine suffocating myself with a plastic bag. I am not sure if the events of the past had something to do with my tendency to think about suicide or if my brain chemistry predisposed me to it.

There was a lot of sexual abuse in my childhood, and one person who abused me a lot. The first time it ever happened, I was about four or five. I had a playmate who was a little older than me. She had Down's Syndrome, and I think someone probably did something to her and she was acting out that behaviour on me. She knew it was wrong. Her mental disability wasn't an excuse, but she did sexually abuse me. I was obviously uncomfortable with what was going on, but I thought little of it. It didn't feel traumatic. In the moment it was awkward and weird and uncomfortable, and I knew it was inappropriate but I never told anybody. It wasn't that the person told me not to say anything. I just knew that certain areas of my body were to remain covered, so I just knew that for some reason I couldn't tell anyone.

I think that's one thing parents can do: tell their children that if anyone ever says anything or touches them inappropriately to always tell someone they trust.

There was also someone close to my family who had abused me for many years. I was about seven at this time. He would perform very explicit sexual acts on me. It started off innocently: hugs that lasted a little too long—nothing explicit. I began to trust him, and then it became very bad. He would say things like, "Don't say anything" and he would blackmail me. If I had told a lie the previous day, he would say things like, "If you say anything, they will think you are lying."

In the beginning, he would tell me not to say anything, but later he didn't have to tell me to keep it quiet. It might have looked like I was a willing participant, but it was just grooming. He was making me be a part of it even though children can never voluntarily be a part of that. The abuse lasted until I was about eleven. When I was younger, the whole thing was very uncomfortable for me, but even then it didn't make me cry or do anything. It was just uncomfortable, especially when I knew that the act was about to start. When the act was over, I'd go back to doing what I was doing. I have no recollection of it being something I thought about. I never dwelled on it during my day. I was still having these weird suicidal thoughts, though, and I was having what they call "stimming," where some people flap their hands or make repetitive movements. I used to do that but one of my family friends has severe autism, and my family thought I was just imitating that person. I am not sure if I was imitating anyone or if I was trying to cope, but I used to do these things and they became more hidden. I was very quiet and introverted. I have never been sure if these things were related to the trauma or if it was my brain chemistry.

My parents had no idea what was going on. They never even suspected anything. I think the only way they would have known is if I had told them.

> My parents had no idea what was going on. They never even suspected anything.

## RELIVING THE TRAUMA

The abuse ended when I was about eleven, but right up to age eighteen, it never really came up in my mind. If I heard someone retell their story or heard statistics about abuse, I'd be like, "Yea, that's happened to me." But that would be the end of it, so it would seem that I was very healthy but I really wasn't. I turned eighteen and went to university, which I didn't find particularly stressful. I had come from a pretty rigorous academic program in high school and should have easily adjusted, but something about that transition triggered a lot of these memories. That's when things became really hard for me.

I'd be in class writing notes, and then I'd suddenly zone out. I'd be having all these flashbacks, and by the time I came back to myself, everyone would be gone and I'd be alone in the lecture hall. It was difficult; I couldn't sleep well. I had nightmares and flashbacks. It was very hard. I didn't think I was stressed out because of university. I was adjusting really well. I felt like I had a lot of freedom, I had my friends from high school and was making new friends, my tuition was paid, and I had no student loans. I didn't have anything stressing me out. But whatever caused it came and it came hard. I know that these sorts of things don't stay buried forever. Maybe something triggered me that I don't even know.

I knew I wasn't in good shape, but I was in denial. I thought of myself as a mental health advocate. I cared about people going through difficult things, but I didn't want to admit that I needed professional help myself. A few months after the beginning of the next semester, I got professional help for the first time, and even then it wasn't consistent. I was just doing it because someone forced me into it. The first time I willingly sought help was about a year later. It was hard. I hadn't understood therapy or how mental health needs treatment, just as one goes to a doctor when sick. I had a bit of a wall up with respect to getting treatment. The treatment helped, but initially I wasn't willing to be vulnerable and put in the effort, so that made things take longer than they should have. Eventually I started to see the benefit. It was a slow process. The trauma was very deep. Even to this day, I'm still working through a lot of things.

## SEEKING THERAPY

In the beginning, I did talk therapy. That meant sitting with a counsellor for about fifteen minutes regularly. My parents were not involved at first, and when they did find out about it they were pretty upset. They didn't know the issues I had and thought that whatever it was—they didn't even know about the abuse at the time—could be solved by prayer and eating better or by getting off my phone or being more obedient. They were not initially very supportive of me getting therapy, which can be very difficult when you are trying to get help.

Parents need to be careful with what they say to their children, especially younger children. When I was young, I remember telling my parents that one of my friends had hurt my feelings. It was something childish but it meant a lot to me. My friend had cheated on a game we were playing, and it wasn't so much that my friend had cheated that hurt me, it was that she had broken my trust. I told my parents that "My friend had hurt my feelings" and they just brushed it off. I don't think it was meant to silence me, but in that specific moment all I remember thinking was that *They don't care about my feelings*. I carried that with me for a very long time.

It's important to realize that everything children say is important to them. Sometimes adults think that children don't understand the world. It's true they don't understand it in the way that adults do, but to a child every little thing is important, so adults shouldn't dismiss these little things no matter how minuscule they seem because their kids are saying what they are saying for a reason. Parents should learn how to listen to their kids. Even if the parents have to shut their kids down, they should never do it in a way that dismisses or invalidates anything they have said. Sometimes it takes kids a lot longer to say what they need to say because they don't have the vocabulary, or they don't know how to speak to adults. Parents need to understand that their kids are people too.

My parents are very good parents. If they had just heard the fact that what was really bothering me was that I felt my friend had betrayed me, they wouldn't have dismissed it. I don't think they would have shut me down for that.

I have worked at a day camp for the past two years, and something the kids really like is that I never shut them down. At the end of the day, as long as we have done the games I planned for them, I just want them to have a good time. Seeing kids be positive or expressive is what I want. There are a lot of things kids say that you won't catch if you don't let them speak. One time, there was this child who was just talking nonstop. I just wanted her to be quiet because I was getting a headache, but I had to keep reminding myself to just let her express herself. As she spoke, she ended up saying something that sounded like she was being abused at home by her grandfather. I reported it to my boss, who reported it to the police, and it was discovered that her grandfather was doing some horrible things to her. I wouldn't have known that if she felt that she wasn't allowed to speak or that she had to be quiet. Sometimes, children will tell you something that you didn't know about them or do something you wouldn't have done at that age. I feel we would do good not to challenge them all the time. There are times when it's good to be quiet and listen.

I still struggle with my own challenges, but the thing that keeps me around is knowing that I have survived one hundred per cent of my worst days. Even on the days when I felt living wasn't worth it, I survived that day, too. That's motivating for me. Not that it takes the pain away or that it makes life easier, but knowing that if I have done it before I can do it again.

> The thing that keeps me around is knowing that I have survived one hundred per cent of my worst days.

Talking and having someone around really helps me cope. Someone who can be there to ask if I need a hug or time by myself. Know what's good for you and adapt it to whatever you need. It helps when you have severe manifestations.

# Chapter 3:
# Avoiding Anger
By A. K, 23-year-old male

I come from a blended family. I'm the oldest of my siblings. Even though my dad is not my biological father, he was there from the beginning, and he is the only father I've ever known. My parents moved to Canada in the late nineties, some years before my brother and I did. They wanted to establish themselves first, so they left us with our grandmother while they got settled.

## REUNITING WITH MY PARENTS

It was about six years later, in 2005, when my brother, grandmother, and I flew to Barrie, Ontario, to join my parents. I had lived with my grandmother for as long as I could remember. I was only three years old when my parents left, so I hadn't lived with them in my formative years. It was a really tough transition. I was almost ten by this time and had no memory of either of them prior to moving to Canada. I had seen pictures of them while in Africa but after being long separated from my parents, Grandma was now "Mom" to me.

It was a very strange dynamic to have my mother and grandma in the same room. When someone disciplines you for six years, and then all of the sudden they take a step back and someone else takes over, it's quite strange. My grandma eventually left me and my brother to go back to Zimbabwe. The first year with my mother in Canada was very tough. I had to adjust so much. If my parents told me they loved me, in my mind

> I had seen pictures of them while in Africa but after being long separated from my parents, Grandma was now "Mom" to me.

I'd be saying, *But where were you for six years?* I adjusted easier to my mom than to my dad, though. My dad and I have very similar personalities: we can be very confrontational. I got more beatings from him than from my mom. I'd say to him, "Why do you keep hitting me if you say you love me?" He would say something along the lines of, "Hitting you hurts more for me." But I'd respond back and say, "You are lying! You are hitting me because you are angry." Even right up to the last couple of years, my relationship with my dad was very rough. It's been the toughest relationship to heal. Things were easier with my mom.

## SEARCHING FOR MY BIRTH FATHER

When I became a teenager, I had to deal with the fact that my dad wasn't my biological father, even though he had been there since my birth. I had lots of unanswered questions about my real father. I wanted to know why he hadn't been there for me. As I grew older, I started to ask questions about him. He died when I was about fourteen. Before that, I had seen him only once when he came to sign over full custody to my mom so that I could come to Canada. I never saw him after. That left a big void in me. I appreciate my adoptive dad now. It was big for someone who never gave "birth" to me to take me in and treat me just like his son. Not every kid gets

> I had lots of unanswered questions about my real father. I wanted to know why he hadn't been there for me.

to have that, sometimes not even from their biological fathers. It's only now that I see how awesome he really is, but before I didn't like him too much.

One time before my real dad passed away, I knew something had happened to him and I kept asking, "Where is he? What's happening?" My mom, in frustration, just yelled, "He is dead!" I was stunned and I remember saying to myself, *Well, I guess that stops that conversation.*

I became quite a difficult kid as a teenager. I started to act out. Some members of my real dad's family reached out to me, but it didn't do anything for me. I'm now connected to my dad here because I now understand what it takes to love a kid who's not biologically yours. Being in a blended family had its challenges. I thought I was my mom's favourite, but I thought my dad didn't like me at all. My dad is a different type of guy. He shows his affection and appreciation by being extra-hard on someone, which to the recipient is not a good thing. In his eyes, I was the kid with the most potential, so he felt he had to push me more.

When we got beatings, I'd count them. If he hit me seventeen times and hit my brother fifteen, I'd know it and ask why. He would say, "It's because you are older." I felt he didn't really like me and because of that, I never cared, and the bad kid in me came out. Because my own biological father had left, I often felt even my adopted father would leave me as well. I'd talk back, I'd drop my pants, listen to rap music, and do anything and everything to get on his nerves. I'd purposely defy him. If he told me to pull up my pants, I pulled them down. I was told I'd never be allowed to pierce my ears, so I got these magnetic earrings just to test him. I felt I was a grown man, and nobody could tell me what to do.

> Because my own biological father had left, I often felt even my adopted father would leave me as well.

For the longest time, our relationship was one of an angry kid and angry father. I've been a Christian since 2016. From that time until now, the mending that should have happened years prior is finally happening now. I never experienced a lot of "I love yous" or hugs or things like that. My dad had his own issues because of his past. His dad didn't really like him, but he went through worse than me. When I put that in perspective and compare it to what I received, he went through genuine abuse. So he passed some of that on to me. As an adult, I can now see that his responses were a reaction to what he had been through. It wasn't so much that he didn't like me. He never got hugs, so he never gave hugs.

My dad first told me "I love you" on his fortieth birthday in front of two-hundred people. I cried so much I don't even remember the rest of the evening. After I got saved as a Christian, I felt the Lord telling me, "Through you, I will change your family. I want you to reflect my love, then they will change." Love is the mark of a Christian.

## Making Sacrifices

I loved to play sports. In Grade 5, I was chosen to play on the junior high basketball team, which was made up of people in grades 7 and 8. By the time I was in grades 7, 8, and 9, I had college basketball scouts looking for me. Basketball was life for me. I gave it one hundred per cent. I'm five foot six, but I had opportunities to play National Collegiate Athletic Association (NCAA) basketball. I slept and ate basketball. I wasn't the smartest kid in school, but I was a hard worker. I had to study three times more than other kids to get good grades. I knew I could get good grades. I just had to study harder. My dad instilled in me a strong work ethic.

From grades ten to twelve, my sights were set on getting into the National Basketball Association (NBA). I knew I wasn't going to be a doctor or lawyer or have a job that was going to pay me a very high salary, so I believed sports was the way out for me. My parents put me in an accelerated program in school, but I'd skip certain classes to go train. I just needed a passing mark, so I'd show up for the bare minimum. I used to take four buses to get to school and stay till 4 p.m. or 5 p.m., when the teacher would open the gym for me. Then I'd do basketball training the rest of the day.

I graduated from high school in 2014 and played semi-pro football with the Edmonton Wildcats until 2016, when I got an opportunity to go to the one NCAA school in Canada. I was sure it was going to work out. Only one school in Canada had that opportunity, and I had gotten accepted. By this time I had such a falling out with my parents, I had already moved out.

Six days before I was to drive out to Vancouver, I broke my right leg during a game. My tendons were shattered, and my kneecap blew up. My brother and best friend took me to the hospital, where I was told that a lot more would have been damaged if it weren't for my muscles, which were pretty strong. I thought I'd be back in a short time, but after a while I started to realize that I was probably never going to play again. I was worried that I'd never walk or run—ever. A few days later, I got sent in for surgery. It was late December, and I remember I called my mom. I hadn't talked to her for months at this point. The first thing my mom said when she heard my voice was, "I thought I'd never hear from you." I had called her because I needed a place to stay. I couldn't live on my own anymore. I was going to be unable to walk for three to four months. My mom was so gracious. She just said, "Absolutely, no problem, come back."

> I picked the school farthest from where they lived, so I'd have no reason to go back to see them.

I had my surgery on Christmas Eve. I was angry. When I left for school, I had promised that I'd never talk to my parents again. I picked the school farthest from where they lived, so I'd have no reason to go back to see them. I had told them, "You guys will never see me again." Calling them after my leg was broken was very emotional for my mom. My whole life and focus had been to play sports, and it had been taken away from me. I had sacrificed: I didn't go to parties, and I had done everything in my power to succeed. It seemed everything I had sacrificed for had been taken away in an instant.

When you sacrifice seven years for a goal, you give up part of your childhood. It becomes an idol, and when that is taken away, you don't know who you are anymore. Basketball was my whole identity. I started to ask really deep questions. I had questions and I knew the answers to my questions had to be somewhere. One morning, I was at a kitchen table around five or six a.m., and I picked up a Bible and read a passage in the book of Matthew that instantly changed me.

I said, "God, if you are real, I need answers because this doesn't make sense." I had nowhere else to turn. It was when I was in a pit that I realized there was more to life than money, wealth, and fame. I started to realize that there was a bigger purpose for my life. I had grown up around religious people, but they all seemed fake. They all said one thing but did the other. I had never come across a genuine Christian and I had a tough time with that.

## HEALING FROM ANGER

After my experience in 2016 at that table, it's all gone: the anger, rebelliousness, and bitterness. I changed radically, and people who knew me couldn't believe it was the same me. They expected me to become my old self, but after a few years, people started to see that the change that had happened was genuine. Some people would ask, "Are you okay, man?"

The hardest part was knowing you have changed but people still see the old person you were. I genuinely meant well for people. But I had spent twenty years taking advantage of them, so even though I had changed, the old me was all people expected. People get suspicious when you genuinely try to be good to them. As I changed, my family also changed. To be in the same room and talking was a miracle in itself.

I believe you don't have to wait for the other person to come and apologize before the relationship can be healed. I saw God work in such a way in my family that I'd come home and cry. Our relationship is not perfect, but it's a hundred times better than it was. The Lord is good.

# Chapter 4:
# Parenting Done Right
By K. C, 27-year-old female

My dad came to Canada for school. Three years later, my mom and I left Ghana and joined him in Quebec. It's been twenty-three years now since we arrived. When we got to Canada, I felt different from other people. I never spoke French or English, so I had a language barrier and struggled to make friends. I eventually enrolled in school and spoke French, but at other places outside school like church, it was English. At home we spoke Twi.

I grew up in the middle of three cultures, but the Ghanaian culture was dominant. We ate Ghanaian food and my parents spoke to me in Twi. I'd eat McDonald's only if there was nothing at home. I grew up very close to my parents, so I feel that helped me not get sucked into peer pressure. I never had a job right up to the end of college, so while my friends were buying their own clothes and having expensive hair, I couldn't have all that,

> I grew up very close to my parents, so I feel that helped me not get sucked into peer pressure.

even though I wanted those things as well. It was only after I started work that I could finally buy the things I wanted. My parents did everything for me and my responsibility was just to go to school.

## LIFE AMONG ITALIANS

I grew up not having many friends and the few friends I had lived far from us. When we first moved to Canada, we lived in an area with lots of Ghanaians. Once I started Grade 3, we moved. I only met other Black people once a week at church, or other Ghanaians at weddings, so there was never time to really develop close friendships. I grew up in a community that was predominantly Italian. There were not many Black people around, and the Italians did things differently. Their kids didn't work while schooling, either. They just studied. I found that a lot of Black kids like me tended to work at an early age to help out their families financially. Some of them came from homes where there were five or six kids, but in the Italian community most people had one or two kids, so the kids didn't have to go to work. Their parents could easily provide for them. I think things would have been different if I had not grown up in that community. I'd have probably done a lot of things with other Black people if I was around them, but I was busy with school. I had a math tutor and was involved in afterschool programs. My parents kept me busy.

## WHAT MY PARENTS DID RIGHT

My parents, even to this day, tell me how much they love me and how proud they are of me. If you don't get that at home, you'll seek it out elsewhere. My parents were not particularly strict. They let us do what we wanted to do as long as we were not harming anyone. They would compensate me for doing well at school. If I got eighty per cent in any of my classes, my dad would buy me something.

I know it's not very typical for parents in an African home to verbally tell their kids that they love them, but mine did. I think my dad going to university here played a role in how he viewed things. He met people of other nationalities. My parents still often tell me how proud they are of me, even though I have now moved out and live alone.

## WHAT MY PARENTS COULD HAVE DONE BETTER

I'd make sure when I start my own family that we have family activities together. We didn't do much of that. We rarely ate dinner together and never took road trips together. The only time we ever went anywhere was when we'd go to Toronto for weddings.

If I were to go back in life, I'd choose the same parents again. I'd be happy to be even five per cent of what they are. I'd like to have what my parents gave me and to even supersede it.

# Chapter 5:
# Fitting in Nowhere
By R. D., 25-year-old female

I am the youngest of three siblings. My dad is from South Sudan, and my mom is Filipino. The age gap between my siblings and me made our childhood dynamic interesting. My sister is six years older than me, and my brother is four years older than me. I was always seen as too young and too naive to question their authority even though they never took it for granted. They would always fight with each other but never with me. I often ended up playing alone; my brother, being a boy, didn't want to play "girly games" with me, while my sister claimed she was too old to play with me. Although I envied the fact that my older siblings were closer in age to each other, they always made time for me. That made me cherish the time I did have with them all the more.

Growing up, I was always the mediator between my mom and my older siblings. They both went through their angsty teenage phases around the same time, so my mom enlisted me to help deal with the influx of rebellious behaviours in the house. It's funny to look back now on how I remained loyal to both my mom and my older siblings during times of disagreement. One specific thing I remember was always finding my brother's Gameboy when my mom would hide it as a form of punishment. Being a more quiet and reserved kid, I was very observant. I knew all my mom's favourite places to hide things and knew she would rotate her hiding spot every now and then.

After fighting with my sister and having his Gameboy taken away, my brother would go to his room, obviously upset. Being the young child I was at the time, I believed the simple solution to make my brother happy again was to give him his Gameboy back. Once my mom was busy, I would check her hiding spots, find my brother's Gameboy, and give it back to him. He would calm down, play for a bit, then give it back to me so I could return it to the hiding spot. Our plan worked beautifully and without fail, until my mom eventually caught me, realizing I had been ruining her disciplinary actions for months.

The worst part about growing up with older siblings is always living in their shadows. Since we all attended the same school from kindergarten to Grade 12, I lived in their shadows for my entire adolescence. Teachers would always joke around and call me the mini version of my older sister or refer to me as my brother's little sister. My siblings, for the most part, knew that this was a touchy subject for me and never teased me about it.

## Navigating Three Cultures

Navigating the different cultures became harder with age. Growing up in a single-parent home, I identified more with my mother's Filipino culture. We attended a majority Filipino church, went to many Filipino-centric events, and had many Filipino family friends. I'm thankful I was able to learn a lot about my culture. But due to that, I also learned a hard lesson early on in life: because of the colour of my skin, I was treated differently than my full Filipino friends or even my half-white, half-Filipino friends. It was the constant microaggressions that really turned me off, like asking where my mom was when she was standing nearby, asking if I liked Filipino food, or asking which friend had brought me to the function.

> *also learned a hard lesson early on in life: because of the colour of my skin, I was treated differently than my full Filipino friends or even my half-white, half-Filipino friends.*

These phrases became normal, but they never stopped hurting. It's hard to be seen as an outsider by your own people. I remember one time I went to a Filipino festival with my Filipino friend, and while waiting in line for food, a lady came up to me, handed me a pamphlet advertising different Filipino business in the city, and told me to give it to any Filipino friends that I may have. Honestly, it hurt a lot to hear that. I can't blame her entirely for not knowing that I am Filipino, but it was the gatekeeping vibes of the interaction that turned me off completely. I went to this festival to experience my culture, yet time and time again, I was continually treated as an outsider.

A difficult thing during my adolescent years was coming to terms with beauty standards. Filipino beauty standards very

> *It was difficult trying to live up to a standard that I could never attain.*

much favour light skin and skinny bodies—of which I have neither. My mother, of course, held those same ideals as well. I can't blame her for planting these ideals in my head, but it was difficult trying to live up to a standard that I could never attain.

In all honesty, I don't have a very strong connection to my African heritage. When I was young, I associated my South Sudanese culture with my father. Because he had left us, I didn't want anything to do with a culture that didn't want anything to do with me. Of course I know better now, but that thought process definitely hindered my willingness to learn and educate myself. I felt like this also affected my ability to make close relationships with my cousins. I felt like I wouldn't be able to connect with them due to my the disconnect with our culture.

Growing up surrounded by your culture is something people shouldn't take for granted. Culture plays a huge role in shaping identity. I felt that I was missing half of who I was, and I still feel that way. I feel like I missed out on a lot by growing up without learning about South Sudanese culture. The more I learn about it now, the more I wish I could've grown up immersed in the culture.

## FINDING MY IDENTITY

Personally, I feel like I identify as Canadian the most. I never felt like I belonged to either Filipino or South Sudanese culture entirely, leaving Canadian as my default choice.

It's an interesting dichotomy; being biracial, I don't feel like I belong to either ethnicity. I felt like an outsider whenever friends would talk about their families and cultures. My heart was hardened to Filipino culture due to the alienation I felt, and I couldn't

> *t's an interesting dichotomy; being biracial, I don't feel like I belong to either ethnicity.*

relate to my African culture because I just didn't know enough about it. In either culture, I felt like I'll always be looked at as a foreigner: never enough to be accepted.

I don't think the challenges I faced were completely unique. When speaking on culture, I think a lot of people who grow up in places like Canada feel a disconnect to their culture to some extent. Growing up in Canada, my mom was very much focused on creating a good life for my siblings and me. The term "whitewashed" was something I heard a lot growing up, but I personally have never felt like I was "whitewashed." This term stems from the judgment of others—people determining whether or not you're connected enough to your heritage. I always wondered why it was such a bad thing to be considered more Canadian, as I was born in and raised in Canada, after all. I feel like sometimes parents expect their children to experience culture in the exact same way that they did growing up, but that's not possible—and that's fine.

Despite experiencing my culture differently, my mom never faulted me for not being more in tune with my culture. She was happy to cook me traditional food and share personal stories but never shamed me for not knowing enough. I feel like this was specifically because I'm biracial; any comments she made would be a bit hypocritical. I could never really share my problems with my friends because I felt they would never understand. It was lonely going through this, believing that I had no one to rely on.

## EMBRACING MYSELF

I had to overcome many hurdles in order to accept myself. I had to unlearn a lot of behaviours and mindsets I had built over the years, a lot of them having to do with self-esteem and identity issues. Navigating three cultures is an interesting experience. Growing up, I felt that I was never Filipino or Sudanese enough to fully claim either culture, but saying I was just Canadian didn't feel right, either. Dating was one area in which I felt extremely self-conscious. I felt that I could never date someone Filipino or South Sudanese due to judgment from their family. In both cultures, choosing a suitable partner your parents approve of is very important. I knew that my mom would never fault me for who I chose, as she was in an interracial relationship, but I feared that wouldn't be enough to appeal to my potential partner's family.

> I hated having to constantly prove to people that I belonged to both cultures, and I wished I could just choose one

There were many times when I was younger that I wished I was just fully one half or the other. I hated having to constantly prove to people that I belonged to both cultures, and I wished I could just choose one. It took a lot of self-reflection and self-assurance to get to where I am today. I can't spend time wishing for a different situation but instead have to love what I have been given.

I always felt the need to connect with my African side, with that need intensifying as I grew older; I always felt like part of me was missing. Seeing my African friends be loud and proud made me a little envious of the experience I could have had. I saw the vibrance of African cultures and felt like I could never be a part of it. My experiences with the Filipino community growing up carried a sense of elitism and bias, and I assumed I would feel the same way if I tried to learn more about my African culture. I know now that it wasn't the Filipino culture but very specific people who carried these views. I definitely feel like there's a specific void that can only be filled by learning about South Sudanese culture.

The secret to my strength is having a firm foundation and a supportive group of people around me. I was lucky to grow up in a church that was accepting and loving, and I was able to create a strong set of core beliefs. This way, I always have something to fall back to, a way to shape my decision-making and focus my thinking. A solid support group is imperative to developing as a person. My friend group is one I have cultivated over the years; we've learned so much about each other and have built trusting relationships with each another. I know I can always count on them to give the hard truth I need to hear, or the nurturing loving I need to heal. I think these two things can ensure that you have the energy to keep pushing through, even when things get extremely difficult.

Lately, I try to live my life by doing things that will make me proud of myself. I don't want to necessarily live without regrets, but I want to live in a way that I can look back and be satisfied with what I've accomplished. It's not only the big things that keep me motivated, but the little things as well. Anticipating the release of the next big movie, planning a future trip with friends, or looking forward to eating new foods are honestly things that keep me going.

# Chapter 6:
# Unending Transitions

By P. J., 26-year-old male

I came to Canada from Zambia in the early 2000s. I was fourteen and had just started secondary school in Zambia, which was already big transition for me. I had hardly settled into secondary school when we moved to Canada. The changes were very hard on me.

When we got to Canada, my whole family was going through major adjustments and figuring out how to cope in our new environment. We had only been tin Canada for a few days when I started school. In Zambia, the school year ran from January to December, while the Canadian school year runs from September to June, so I didn't neatly fit in. I was pushed to be ahead of where I had left off in Zambia in order to be in class where Canadian kids my age were. There was no chance to adapt, and things moved too fast for me.

## FITTING IN AT SCHOOL

I was the only Black kid in school. That didn't affect me much, but one thing that almost immediately struck me was how less-defined space between guys and girls is among

39

teens. In Zambia, at those ages, guys and girls barely mingled, but in Canada guys and girls were always together. I found I suddenly had to relate to the opposite sex a lot more than I had before. I'd see boys and girls openly kissing in school. That was something you would never see happen in Zambia, even among adults. Relationships are much more out in the open in Canada. Even the expectations of what it means to be in a relationship are completely different. In Zambia, I never felt I would not be dating for a very long time but in Canada, just about all kids my age dated. There was pressure to fall in line and do what everyone else did. Learning how to react and cope with all these new changes and challenges added a certain amount of stress on me. I found myself very reluctant to assimilate, and I was skeptical of my new environment.

In class I remember one time I wanted to solve a problem in math and asked my teacher a question, which led to me being put through a full assessment of my math ability. That was confusing to me because I just wanted an answer to a problem. My parents became concerned when they heard about it, because they thought I was falling behind and failing my math class. So I was now dealing with the issue both in school and at home, and that was stressful. At the time, I felt that there was something wrong with the way I was approaching everything. I had an older brother who seemed to have adapted easily to Canada, both in his studies and his social life, perhaps because he was a little older and more mature than I was. But for me, the transition was hard. I often felt I was going through it all by myself.

In hindsight, I think what would have helped would have been to have space when we arrived. It would have been nice to just have some time to settle in. Having better communication to talk about what we were all going through as a family would have helped too. But life is never perfect, so I know it couldn't have happened exactly that way now that I look back.

> *In hindsight, I think what would have helped would have been to have space when we arrived.*

## MOVING AGAIN

Within a year of arriving in the small prairie town where we lived, we moved to a bigger city. Things had just started to settle down for me, and this change to a new city was too much for me to handle. I felt I needed to get out of school for a while. I needed to focus on the things that made me happy. Some people adapt and assimilate, but I went the opposite direction. My need to find space led me to dig deeper into the thing that I enjoyed, which was art. In art, I found a quiet space from everything that was going on.

Taking that two or three years to focus on my art helped me cope with the pressure that I had been going through. I wanted nothing to do with school. I just wanted do something I cared about. After about three years of focusing on myself, I decided to re-enter the world as an art student. Unfortunately, art college wasn't what I thought it would be. There were sacrifices I had to make in order to be a successful artist and pursue a career in this field, and I wasn't ready to make them. Even though that did not work the way I wanted, doing what I liked helped me find balance.

I also enjoyed doing things in church, which was different compared to what it was in Africa. But my faith kept me from becoming reckless and getting into drugs or abusing alcohol as many others tend to. I was also trying to live up to the expectations my family had for me and my own expectations of myself. I always believed I could do something useful with my life. I truly believed that God wanted me to go through everything I was passing through and that I could get through it without destroying myself. I didn't want to disappoint my family. I wanted to prove that I was capable of succeeding.

> *always believed I could do something useful with my life*

## BEING A YOUNG BLACK MALE

It's not easy for many young Canadian minorities to find their identity in this culture. In places like high school, people celebrate you for what you can do well. Being a foreign kid, you look for that one thing that people can praise you for or the thing that makes you feel special outside your skin colour. Many times, that thing is music or athleticism. I think that's why so many young immigrants gravitate towards those things. It's really an issue of self-worth. Perhaps that's easier to do than constantly feel the need to prove your intelligence to teachers who sometimes question your capabilities and abilities.

Kids end up doubling down on music and sports because in North America those things are celebrated especially in the media. Many immigrant parents see a career in music or sports as a negative thing, and the first reaction they have when their child expresses an interest in becoming a musician or athlete is to kick the interest out of their child and prevent them from going down those paths. I think the children need to be allowed the experience, but parents need a strategy on how to approach their child's education at the same time. Life has its way of teaching one to be pragmatic. Sometimes, parents should let their children learn as they go and be there to guide when the child makes a mistake. I advise young people to first focus on what's needed as far as a career is concerned, then enjoy their creative side. Education will give them something to fall back on.

> Kids end up doubling down on music and sports because in North America those things are celebrated especially in the media.

Parents should not try to destroy their kids' creativity but also should not completely let them do whatever they want. There needs to be a balance. Eventually, the thing that the child will be most successful at will take over. By the time they are in their twenties, most kids generally figure things out. When a child turns eighteen or nineteen, parents have to realize that they can't completely control them. Sometimes children rebel because they want to maintain their independence and sense of worth. In my case, the more people pushed against what I was doing, the more I felt I had to do it. To me, I felt like everyone

> When a child turns eighteen or nineteen, parents have to realize that they can't completely control them.

was trying to take away one of the very few things I was enjoying. Sometimes a child feels he has to do what he is doing in order to prove his parents wrong. But once you don't feel like you have to compete with your parents, you won't be as reckless with your decisions and actions.

## PLANNING FOR MY FUTURE

My future isn't as clear as I'd like it to be. My decisions in the past still affect me today. For now, I am taking more school and working, but I still hope to do some of the things that I am passionate about. I believe I am more mature now and will make more balanced choices today than I would have in the past. I am being pragmatic about my decisions, but I haven't given up on the things I love.

Young people should not be afraid to recognize what they are going through. We don't talk much about mental health as immigrants, but it's a very important area that should not be ignored. Families should talk about mental health. They should be able to recognize and admit when they are going through challenging times and acknowledge what each person is experiencing. Sometimes families face pressure to look perfect, but they should be willing to give each other time and space and accept that failure is okay sometimes. We are never defined by our failures.

# Chapter 7:
# Finding Myself

By P. C., 27-year-old female

Our home was a mix of both Canadian and East African culture. I was so young when we moved, so I was exposed to Canadian culture more heavily than I was to my parents' culture. We ate the things we would eat in Africa, like potatoes, beans, rice, and chapati. My parents spoke our language between themselves but allowed us to use English so we could communicate with the rest of the world. My parents were very vigilant with surrounding us with African people so my siblings and I were not completely engrossed in Canadian culture.

## A Battle Between Two Worlds

Figuring out who I am has been a battle my whole life. Culture-wise, I am still very much African, but I have been in Canada for so long that I have adapted a lot of Canadian customs. There are things in East African culture that I don't agree with. For example, how women have to cater to men's wishes. As someone who has grown up in Canada where there is a lot of women's freedom and women's equality, I lean towards Canadian culture.

In East African culture, respect is very important. No matter who the person is or how they treat you, you are expected to respect them. That can be very toxic, especially if you are being abused and you can't say or do anything about it. Canadian culture teaches you to be assertive, to stand your ground, and if you are being disrespected, you let someone know. That's something I struggled with growing up. I tend to avoid the person rather than deal with the situation.

## An African and Religious Upbringing

The household I grew up in is both very African but also very religious, so when there were issues I had to handle, I was usually dealing with both culture and religion. The majority of African parents can be very black and white on issues and can be very judgmental. My parents believe if things are not going well for you, then you are wrong and you need to change your attitude or perspective. In my home, whenever I had issues, I would just deal with whatever was happening on my own without informing my parents.

> In my home, whenever I had issues, I would just deal with whatever was happening on my own without informing my parents.

If a situation happened at school that I was not happy about, for example if I went to my parents and told them I was being bullied, the first question from them would be, "What were you doing to cause people to bully you?" I would always be blamed for whatever happened to me. They always assumed that I must be doing something wrong for people to treat me a certain way. Life isn't like that, but in our home my parents always believed in the biblical adage, "You reap what you sow." If bad things are happening to you, then it's you who has planted a bad seed, so to say. In those moments as a child, I wanted to hear the words, "Oh, I am sorry for what you are going through," or something comforting. Because of that, I would just deal with whatever was going on around me on my own. The last place I would bring issues to would be my parents because they would make me feel something wrong with me.

I am not sure that will ever change. I am grown up now, but it's so ingrained in my head not to talk to my parents about issues because I feel they would still respond the same way today. If I was to become a parent, I think I would be more similar to my mother. My mom and dad grew up very differently, and they adopted the parenting styles that their own parents used. My dad is typical African. His approach is, "You do what I say without any questions, whys, or buts. I am always right. You can argue with me but in the end you will still do what I want." My dad had a very hard time with me and my siblings because we grew up here in Canada, and in this culture, you stand your own ground. He could not deal with us asking, "Why?"

My mom will tell you what she wants and doesn't want and then leave you to make your own decision. I think that style worked better for me. I'm a curious person, and the only way for me to learn something is for me to fail at it. With my dad, because he told me "no" all the time, I would end up doing the very things he didn't want me to do anyway. Mom would let

> **With my dad, because he told me "no" all the time, I would end up doing the very things he didn't want me to do anyway.**

me make mistakes, and in the end I'd realize why she had been saying no previously.

In our household, image was very important. Presenting a perfect picture to the outside world was very important. "Don't embarrass" us was the motto of our home, so I find myself anxious about living up to those expectations, and I find myself more comfortable around children because they are not judgmental. I'm always thinking in my head, *Is what I am doing going to be negatively affecting my self-image or my family?* I'm always trying to paint myself into this picture they created and it has affected my self-image. I tend to do things just to please people, even if it's going to affect me negatively. If I'm in a work situation, I tend to avoid seeking promotions or positions of leadership because I feel like I have to please everyone, which I can't do in those positions.

On the other hand, I also tend to be more compassionate and sympathetic. If my friends are in the middle of a difficult issue, often I am able to help them see the issue from a different perspective. My parents are very hospitable people and have raised me to be helpful towards others. For example, my dad will always invite new people he meets at church to our home, and my mom is always cooking for people.

## A GENERATIONAL AND CULTURAL DIVIDE

In most African homes, the generational and cultural divide really hurts the relationship between parents and their kids. Parents usually hold on to their culture, but the kids are a mixture of cultures. My parents grew up in East Africa with their ways of doing things, but when they use those methods on me here, it doesn't always work because I am growing up in a different environment. If I were to say to my mom, "I don't want to get married," she would be very confused to hear that because that's completely different from how she grew up. We all like our comfort zones. My parents are comfortable with the way they grew up and all this is very new to them. Kids from similar backgrounds see that and conclude their parents are judgmental, so they rebel or do things in secret. I find that happens in a lot of families in which parents are very strict. In homes where there is a better balance, parents are aware that there are things they don't understand and they allow their children to find themselves instead of trying to put what they know onto their children. A lot of parents make the mistake of just saying, "This is what I know and this is what you will do."

## BEING YOUNG, BLACK, AND FEMALE

Generally speaking, Black people who have largely grown up in Africa and Black people who have largely grown up in the West see racial matters quite differently. My parents, for example, do not see the point of celebrating things like Black History Month. It's different for them. I think it is harder to be black here in North America than it would be in Africa. It is true that racism here is not as in your face as it once was; now it comes in subtle forms. For example, in social media and just about everywhere you go, the way beauty is presented is very white. For children growing up and looking at beauty in the media and not seeing themselves represented, they think they are not beautiful, that they are not worthy.

> *For children growing up and looking at beauty in the media and not seeing themselves represented, they think they are not beautiful, that they are not worthy.*

Every Black young woman I know has struggled with self-image. Then in the workplace, I feel like I have to go looking and presenting myself as close as possible to a white woman. That means I can't wear my hair naturally, and I have to act and talk a specific way. I have to be quiet, basically because Black women are seen as being loud and aggressive. I can't express my opinions because I'd be seen as being rude and mean. Added to that, my culture also teaches that children are to be quiet and sit; it can be a bad combination.

The subtle forms of racism now are also psychological, so when I see things happening in places like the US, it sparks rage in me. Even though it's not me being killed, I still go through similar situations. I still get followed around in malls and get the occasional racist comment. It's hard to live in a world where you are not the standard for beauty and can never be. It would definitely be easier in a place where everyone looks like you. I try to surround myself with people who have similar backgrounds and experiences to me, so that way whenever anything happens, I have someone to talk to and laugh about it with. It helps ease the situation. When I went to university, I was around a lot of African students who had similar experiences with parents, school, and racial matters, and it helped me be more comfortable to be myself. I am not sure who I am yet, but because I am with people who are similar, I am able to find myself a little bit better.

# Chapter 8:
# Healing Wounds

By L. M., 23-year-old-female

My journey with depression started when I was about fourteen. I was nine when we arrived in Canada. My dad arrived in Canada a few years before the rest of us and it was a little awkward being all together again. My parents were constantly fighting. They fought for as long as I can remember, even before we moved to Canada. Being in Canada only made things go from bad to worse. I remember my mom being abused physically even when I was young as five. I did not like how my dad was treating my mom and that made me very angry. With time, the anger inside of me changed to sadness. In many African households as a child, you can't say anything. Your opinion doesn't matter. My anger grew and eventually formed into a mental illness. I was angry with both my parents, but I was especially angry with my dad when I got into my teenage years.

> **I did not like how my dad was treating my mom and that made me very angry.**

## The Start of My Mental Health Battles

I started to think a lot of what had been happening over the years. Whenever I saw my dad fight my mom, it triggered those memories from the past before he had left us for Canada. I was very vocal about how I felt, and I was never afraid to verbalize it. I wasn't the typical African kid who watched and kept quiet. I would tell my dad that what he was doing was wrong, and I didn't like how he was treating my mother. Because of my talking, my dad and I would fight a lot. He would say things back to me that made me really angry, but eventually I would just get sad because he said things a father should never say to a daughter.

I became depressed but never sought any professional help because I did not know what was going on inside me. I did not know that there was such a thing as mental health. I could feel a change within me mentally, but my parents just thought I was being moody. In our household, the attitude was "Get over it," but it became something that was affecting me every day. I wanted to beat up my dad. I was very aggressive. I was praying every day that my parents would divorce. I was happy when they fought because in my mind, I figured that the more they fought, the quicker the marriage could be over. I started considering suicide when I was about sixteen. I started to have thoughts of ending my life, and over a period of three months, the thoughts intensified. It was almost as if someone was talking to me telling me to just take my life. I eventually attempted to end my life. When that happened, it startled my

> It was almost as if someone was talking to me telling me to just take my life.

family and they started to take what was going on in me seriously. That was what made them realize that I was not doing okay mentally. My attempt to take my life wasn't done to gain sympathy. At the time, I truly wanted to go. I had no strength to keep going.

## THE ROAD TO HEALING

One good thing that came out of that unfortunate episode was that my mother became more involved with my life. She wasn't the typical African parent anymore. We saw doctors, we went to counsellors, and she did what she could to make sure I got the help I needed. She did a really good job when it came to my mental health. My dad still didn't care: he thought I was just looking for attention. I was prescribed medication for depression and anxiety. I felt my depression was worsening with the pills, so I stopped taking them. In the end, my mother was my most helpful therapist. She was a big part of my healing. She spent a lot of time with me and listened to me. It's quite rare for an African parent to listen to her child but she did. She would ask if I wanted to vent and talk about things. She had completely changed. I could see she really didn't want to lose me or take a chance on me again, and she did everything in her power to make me feel loved and needed. She did a really good job.

I am still on the journey to healing. I love living in Canada, but there is something about being home in Africa: the sun, birds, animals, and trees really help me when I'm there. I have gone through most of my trauma in Canada, so in a way I associate Canada with those traumas. I consider myself to be blessed to be in Canada. I still see a therapist from time to time.

School helps me keep busy, and that helps me manage my mental health. I am still a very depressed and angry person, and it's the anger that's still eating me up inside.

Every day I wake up, I want to turn my anger into something beautiful. I want to do something to help kids in the future. Kids should never have to grow up the way I did. It was traumatic. In the short-term, I want to finish school. I don't want this episode to put me back or to define who I am.

> Every day I wake up, I want to turn my anger into something beautiful.

For someone else who has been through trauma or abuse, I'd say constantly remind yourself of the end goal. You might feel stuck or clouded with darkness and feel like you will not make it to tomorrow, but look forward as much as you can because it will get better. Things will open up for you that you would have never imagined.

# Questions and Answers

with Dr. Ayanda Chakawa, PhD,
Clinical Psychologist

**Why does there seem to be a disconnect between immigrant parents and their children in understanding each other?**

There seems to be this big disconnect between parents and children in first-generation immigrant families, but it's important to recognize that there will always be a generational gap between parents and their children even when they haven't dealt with migrating to a new country. Being immigrants can make things even more challenging, but the key thing is for parents to learn to be sensitive to their children and to realize that every child is different. Even within a culture there are a lot of differences among people, so even people who have experienced the same type of stress may respond differently. Parents should not expect that one child will respond the way others have. Being sensitive to those differences is really important. Parents need to recognize that the Canadian context is different than where they might have come from, so the parent's experiences while growing up in a different country will be different to their kids'.

It is true that there are unique stressors that children in immigrant families experience, and it is important for people not to be dismissive of that. Taking time to listen to your children without judgment shows sensitivity. It's important for parents to recognize that brushing off or dismissing the problem that a child brings to them doesn't resolve the problem. While the parent might think the problem is gone by not addressing it, the child now has to learn how to figure out a solution to the problem on their own. The child will learn that his or her parents may not respect the things that he or she finds challenging and will start to keep certain things to him or herself. That child may not have the tools to figure out that problem and may end up left struggling with something that he or she may not be able to handle.

Problems don't go away by ignoring them. If it was something that didn't seem like a big issue at the time, that issue will still come up in one form or the other. If there wasn't an effective way of dealing with the problem or identifying strategies to navigate that situation previously, then that child is now ill-equipped when a similar situation arises in the future. The child learns to handle things by being secretive or solving the problem in ways that can be harmful.

**Do people go through more mental health challenges in the Western world compared to the developing world?**

That's a tough one. I agree that there does seem to be a higher incidence of mental health challenges here in the West than in the developing world. But just because it seems to be the case doesn't necessarily mean that it is. There are multiple things to consider when looking at this question. Broadly speaking, lower-income countries, for the most part, do not have the same way of tracking data as Western countries when it comes to issues of mental health. So it is quite difficult to make an apples to apples comparison. On one hand, it ends up being based on anecdotal evidence[1] and on whatever the population data shows if there has been research done in that area. There is also less attention given to mental health concerns in developing countries, so it's hard to know how many people are coming in for treatment or intervention. Similar to the Western nations, the rate of mental health concerns is much higher than what the access to treatment is, so there are a lot of unmet and unreported mental health issues and needs.

The immigration experience can also be quite stressful when people have to acculturate to a new environment and that can also contribute to increased mental stress. There is data that shows that when people migrate to North America, a lot of the stress caused by the moving experience contributes to mental health challenges. So on one hand there are unique stressors that contribute to mental health challenges in the West, but because of the stigma around mental health in developing countries, there is a higher level of secrecy when it comes to mental health issues, broadly speaking. Some of that stigma towards mental health issues in developing countries is partially due to lack of awareness, so people may not always see a mental health challenge when it's there.

---

1    Anecdotal evidence is information that may not be completely
     accurate as it relies on observations rather than data and facts.

Also, this culture places different demands and expectations on people that might be different from those in places immigrants come from. Just because the diagnosis isn't given doesn't mean that the concerns aren't there. For example, in some countries, the educational system tracks kids early on solely how they perform academically. Those kids who might be struggling with attention deficit, or learning concerns are just seen as less capable, while the learning or mental health condition is never addressed.

One other consideration relates to awareness. When people talk freely about anxiety or depression, people start to self-reflect when they experience some of those things. But when the conversation isn't really happening widely socially, people's awareness isn't there and people may not necessarily recognize that they are struggling with something that has a name. The awareness difference between countries also contributes to how the issues are being labelled, discussed and treated.

To a certain extent, I would agree that different societies have different ways of managing these issues. Sometimes it may seem like mental health is managed well enough, but you see issues come out in other ways like problems with substance abuse in a society, for example. People in one society might say, "That person is a drunkard," but in this society we are more likely to say, "That person has a substance abuse issue and needs to go and detox." The classification systems are very different. I don't know if the rates of mental issues are as different as what they seem to be.

## What can people do to develop a healthier self-image?

I encourage parents to speak positive messages to their children. Some cultures do not really promote finding things that you can praise someone for, but telling a child that "You are enough, you are beautiful, your hair is beautiful" is really important. Sometimes parents end up sending negative messages to their children without intending to when they say things like, "Your hair is so hard to manage" or things like that. All of that can chip away at your child's self-worth, so positive messages coming from the parents are important. Once the child starts to move into adolescence, that child needs to be empowered to find ways to take ownership and find those positive messages, even if they don't necessarily come from one's parents. These are some preventative measures parents can take.

Sometimes people say, "Just focus on the inner beauty" but that's not the reality, especially for adolescents. If there are ways that parents can help support that process for their girls' self-development, I think that's important. While the goal is not to raise proud kids, having self-confidence is important, and it contributes to healthy and adaptive development.

For young people who are already in this mindset, it is important to understand what is getting in the way of you seeing yourself as important enough. Is it the media or messaging that you are getting socially? That needs to be identified. You need to set up a network for opposite influences to reverse those negative messages and nurture the traits and abilities that contribute to recognizing your worth and uniqueness. Celebrate your version of beauty based on the traits that you have, and also identify positive role models who share similar aesthetics to you and reflect realistic standards.

If there are specific barriers to feeling comfortable with who you are on the outside, such as lack of confidence, it is important to take time to know how to choose clothing or hairstyles that highlight your natural beauty and find examples, explore, and seek out advice on those styles that suit you.

**In many non-Western cultures people are raised to be humble and to defer to their elders, but in North America traits like assertiveness and confidence are often the basis for promotion. How does an immigrant balance these conflicting ideals?**

In non-Western cultures, we are taught to exercise deference even in how we communicate non-verbally. We don't do a whole lot of eye contact because it can be seen as intimidating or lack of respect, whereas in North America eye contact is key. The two different cultural presentations are usually what are referred to as individualistic versus collectivist. Whereas Western culture has a more individualistic orientation and non-Westernized societies have what we would refer to as collectivist orientation, both have merit and both have strengths, so it's about balance. Sometimes we try to pit the two approaches against each other instead of recognizing that there is value in both. The question should be how to marry the two in order to maximize the pros.

Being humble isn't bad and neither is being compliant, whether it's to an adult or to someone older. But where it becomes a problem is when it happens at the expense of not being able to develop a personal value set or when there is no bravery to communicate those values in a respectful way or navigate situations in a way that one can feel confident in.

You also have to remember that there are personality differences. Some will naturally be shyer in certain situations but, that said, you still want kids to feel confident to navigate situations so that they can achieve their desired outcomes. I think it's important to move away from expecting kids to just be followers of adults and generic rule followers. Sometimes, kids are raised just to follow rules, and when the child turns eighteen, he or she is suddenly expected to magically learn independence and advocacy skills. These skills need to be learned at home and, again, it's about balance. Parents can learn how to engage in tough conversations, even within the home, and help the child understand why certain values and expectations are in place for their families. That's critical thinking and helps children develop their own set of values, which they will further develop when they leave the home.

**What are some things you suggest that people can do to ease the transition into this society?**

It can be different approaches, depending on the age, but for parents who migrate with children who are younger, it is important to expose them to a number of different things, academically, musically, and athletically. That all helps to contribute to holistic development. In that context, children's interests and personality will really begin to emerge, and both the parent and child will start to see things that the child can be really good at.

Individuals who do not have that opportunity and come in later in life sometimes get pigeonholed into doing what can get them the most money the quickest so the opportunity to choose and do what they are really passionate about is thwarted in those situations. But self-development never should stop at any stage in life. It is important to identify what one really enjoys and is passionate about and not just be thinking, "What do I think will make the most money for me?" It is important to establish positive peer support, get a role model who is doing things that seem to be beyond the scope of what you would have thought possible, because there is opportunity to learn in those settings. Community and church groups, for example, can be a great setting for that as well, because there can be a lot of diversity in what people are doing in that context. I'd also advise people to limit social media and general media if they notice it constantly feeding them negativity. When people feel pigeonholed, it can fuel mental health issues because people are doing things they are not passionate about and feel like they are just in the grind and get stressed out in the process.

**How can immigrant parents teach their values to their kids, while at the same time allow them to properly integrate into Western culture?**

In psychology, there is something called racial ethnic socialization, which has to do with the what parents say and do to teach their children about their racial/ethnic group as well as how to relate to those who may not be of their same group. Within this field there is something called cultural socialization, which has shown among the best outcomes over time. This strategy involves teaching children culture and values through engaging ways—through art, stories, music, games, and language, rather than lectures. Parents can teach explicitly through things like having discussions about cultural issues or implicitly through things like having cultural items or cultural foods in the home. Doing that helps the child to foster one's sense of identity within their culture. In this way it becomes not just the parent's culture, but the child feels like that's who he or she is as well and takes a sense of ownership within that.

When a parent says things like, "Just do it because I said so," or promotes mistrust towards other groups, it often leads to other problems. It's the parents who chose to make the move here, so the important thing is for them to figure out how to preserve and celebrate their cultures while at the same time recognizing that acculturation needs to take place and helping children navigate through it. If there are messages being taught at school that contradict what the family stands for, parents need to talk about that as a family. They need to explain why, as a family, they want to do things a particular way and ask all family members for their input. Engaging children in the conversation is very important.

Like mentioned before, not talking about things doesn't mean that the issue is not there. We need to take the opportunity to guide children through that process of critical thinking for the differences in things that contradict the family's values. Avoid painting everything with one broad brush. When people say, "Those people are like this or that," then kids don't know how to think through issues because the right way wasn't modelled for them.

**Sometimes tensions build in immigrant families leading to hurt and broken family relationships. For someone looking to find healing, where can somebody start on the road to healing broken family relationships?**

There are a lot of factors to consider. Firstly, what is contributing to the desire to reconcile? It is important to define what the goal of wanting to repair or reunify is, not because you need to justify wanting to reconcile, but understanding what the objective is before going into it is important because it can help guide how one approaches it. For example, if someone is about to be married or has kids and wants to introduce them to family, that can look very different than someone who is alone and had a big fallout with his or her parents and wants to discuss it. The approach can be very different depending on the situation.

Then the person also needs to identify what led to the breach in the relationship and to figure out if they are now ready to accept the things that led to the breach in the first place. Going back into the situation without unchanged perspectives or expectations could just lead to further harm in the relationship. The simple answer is, "Just send a message and start talking." But I think there needs to be some thought given ahead of time to process through the reasons why you want to reconcile, what the expectations are, what you hope to get out of it, and if it doesn't go the way you are hoping, how you plan to communicate boundaries in a healthy way, as well as how to cope with that. It takes preparation.

# Part 2:
# The Immigrant Experience
# and Post-Traumatic Stress

The following stories are taken from individuals who endured the horrors of experiencing war as children. These individuals walked thousands of kilometres in the night over landmines and among wild animals with no shelter or food. They witnessed death, escaped death, and experienced many horrors children should never be exposed to—right until Canada opened its doors to them. These stories will retrace those journeys and will tell how these individuals dealt with the resulting trauma.

In much of non-Western society, there is no vocabulary for the term for post-traumatic stress disorder (PTSD). If at all it ever comes up, it is viewed as a "white people's thing," a phenomenon that only happens to soldiers from Western countries when they return home after fighting in a war. It is rarely recognized as a condition that the immigrant experiences, yet the effects of PTSD are clearly observable in behaviours such excessive outbursts of anger, irritability, depression, violence and, in more extreme cases, substance abuse and suicide.

Fortunately, not all lives of people who have passed through the horrors of war end in disaster; many have lived to thrive and become upstanding citizens and have contributed greatly to their communities. We can learn from these experiences and draw lessons that our families and communities can adopt to support those experiencing these issues.

# Chapter 9:
# Walking a Thousand Miles

By Athiann (real name used with permission),
approximately 40-year-old male

I am the third of six children. I was born between 1977 and 1983 in the country that is now known as South Sudan. But due to lack of records, the exact date of my birth is not known. My name means "to hide." It was given to me because I was born during a time of war, and my parents were trying to hide me so that I wouldn't be killed. Sometime in the mid-1980s, my uncle who was living in Ethiopia came and spoke to the village elders asking if he could take some children back there for school. The elders sat down to pick who would go, and I was among those selected. My uncle returned to Ethiopia alone. A few years later, he came back to get me and some of my cousins to start school in Ethiopia.

We had schools in South Sudan, but they were not very good and forced students to learn Arabic up to high school. My uncle wanted to take us to a place where we could start learning English sooner. The Sudanese government also had a policy of enforcing Sharia law on everybody, including on the Christians in the south.

## LEAVING FOR ETHIOPIA

While we were waiting for my uncle to come back, our village was attacked. Crops were stolen, and homes were burned down. I lost an uncle in that tragedy. It was 1988 when my uncle returned from Ethiopia to take us back there for school. We set off from South Sudan on foot and had to walk through the night among wild animals so that we could not be seen by the enemy airplanes. If your foot hit a stone, there was no stopping. We walked about 1,000 kilometers. There were children as young as five years old among us. It took us four months to cross between the border of South Sudan and Ethiopia. Survival on the journey was difficult. My uncle would speak to the chiefs of the surrounding villages, asking them to prepare some food for us, but that would only last so long. Things got very difficult when we crossed the South Sudan border. The only way we survived was by catching wild animals and eating them.

> The only way we survived was by catching wild animals and eating them.

We arrived in Ethiopia around January 1989 and were taken to a refugee camp. There were many groups in the refugee camp, all of them full of children ranging from the ages of ten to nineteen. Our school was going to be at the refugee camp which was run by the United Nations (UN). My uncle left us there and went to Addis Ababa (the Ethiopian capital) where he was working with the Sudan People's Liberation Army (SPLA). Conditions in the refugee camp were difficult, but we got the chance to go to school and learn English. Young kids had to fend for themselves. Thankfully for us, we had an aunt who stayed a little distance from where we were. She would come to feed me and my cousins from time to time. It was only later that I discovered that the school we were attending was trying to train us as child soldiers. Although the refugee camp was run by the UN, some SPLA agents would come in to train us on how to fight. Their plan was that when we got older, we would go out to fight in the war raging in South Sudan.

**FLEEING FOR LIFE**

We stayed in the camp for three years until Mengistu, the Ethiopian leader, told the SPLA leader to remove all Sudanese refugees from Ethiopia. When my uncle heard the message, he came right away to move us; he knew that our safety was no longer assured in Ethiopia. We went to the border town of Ethiopia and South Sudan and stayed there for almost a year. There was severe hunger in that area. People ate anything that moved, including vultures, to survive.

Many of those who did not leave Ethiopia at that time died, but even in the place we were, we were soon attacked. Bombs were dropped, and the local people in the area were mobilized against us. We eventually moved into the interior of South Sudan and stayed there for three or four months. Some trucks would occasionally come in from Kenya to bring in food, and my uncle decided that it was best for us to leave the area. He arranged to have us get on one of the trucks. We split up into two groups: my aunty, three of her children, me, and two of my cousins in one group, and my uncle and a few others were in the second group. Our group got into a truck while my uncle's second group remained. The plan was to meet up at some point along the way.

We ended up in a town near the border of South Sudan and Kenya while we waited for my uncle's group. They only arrived after a month but word soon got out that a number of us were in the town, so we had to flee for our safety. We got on another truck and moved to a town where we stayed for two months. At this point, going back to our homeland had become impossible, and our only chance of survival was in crossing over into Kenya. We walked for two days, arriving at a Kenyan border town around January 1992, where we stayed for two months. My uncle's life was under threat, and he petitioned the UN for protection. The UN eventually came in and took us to a town called Kakuma, in Kenya. They housed us for a short time but they had planned to have us moved back to South Sudan. When my uncle found out, we set off on foot to go to another town about 400 kilometers away. We spent about four days in the bush walking. On the fifth day, someone offered us a ride, but instead of taking us to our destination, the person took us to the police. The UN eventually found out about what had happened to us and decided to house us just outside the UN compound and gave us a security guard to keep us safe.

## COMING TO CANADA

Between 1997 to 2000, there was an opportunity for us to go to Australia. The Australian government only wanted six people at the time. Since there were eight of us, and my uncle would not leave any of us behind, he turned the offer down. We applied to the US, Sweden, Norway, and Denmark but we were rejected everywhere. We stayed in Kenya right until 2003 when the Canadian government offered all Sudanese people in the camp the chance to come to Canada. We hadn't submitted an application to come to Canada. The government just came and made the offer to us. Because of the tribal tensions, some of the different tribal groupings were sent to Winnipeg, while others were sent to Edmonton. We were originally supposed to go to Winnipeg, but the UN decided to send us to Edmonton instead. It was April 2004 when we arrived in Edmonton, Canada.

There was still snow on the ground when we arrived. We were taken to the Catholic social services, where I did a language assessment. I did well and was given the go ahead to apply to college because my English was good. We had to spend the first year in Canada without work. If we decided to work, we could only make $200 a month. We were each being given about $650 a month for one year and a loan of $3,000 to help us assimilate and settle in. My first job was at a steel bucket–manufacturing company. I had never held a job before, and it was tough work, but I slowly got the hang of it. I enrolled at Norquest College and did two years of upgrading there. From there, I was told I could apply to any university I wanted. A lady from Norquest suggested that I "Just go and work in a warehouse" since I could speak English. Another suggested that I enroll in a small college and not waste time going to university but I had my mind set on university. I went to MacEwan University (MacEwan College at the time) for a year, and then I applied to the University of Saskatchewan, University of Alberta, and the University of British Columbia. I got accepted to the University of

Saskatchewan, in Saskatoon, to study and completed a degree in civil engineering there.

## DEALING WITH TRAUMA

Post-traumatic stress disorder affected all of us that came. When we started living in Canada, things were very different. It was the first time in my life I had ever stayed indoors for six months. We had been used to being out playing and doing different things. For all the years prior to coming to Canada, everything I had been through hadn't affected me. I witnessed fighting, the killing of my own uncle, and other very traumatic experiences, but none of the effects of those things were apparent until I went to school. Then I suddenly started to have all these flashbacks. I'd begun to relive the memories of the past. It was as if I was back in the same place. The emotions were raw. I'd cry easily, and things looked hopeless. I couldn't see beyond the next day. If it wasn't for my faith in God, perhaps I'd have also killed myself like many others did, perhaps I'd have used drugs to help me cope, like many others did. There were some anti-depressants that were given to us when we arrived, but they didn't help me. All those emotions suppressed for years came out, and I didn't know what to do with all those suppressed emotions.

> It was the first time in my life I had ever stayed indoors for six months.

For me, I credit my success in navigating that time to God. I always prayed for Him to help me. I did that, and I wrote poetry. Poetry became part of my healing process. I wrote about everything I had gone through, and I felt better when I wrote it out. Writing and praying really helped me. I also had the courage to say, "This medication isn't good for me." In the camp, I had seen my own cousin kill himself—he just took a knife and cut his throat. He was under those medications and it was so painful to see. I knew that could have easily been me. I chose not to take the medication, but instead I spent time praying, playing, being with others, and writing out what I was going through. I knew I was anxious and stressed, so I prayed about it and I tried to do things that other people would do. I went camping and did sleepovers at our church with my new friends. Having people who loved me and cared for me helped me forget some of what I had gone through.

Coming from the background I had, if someone talked about love, it just didn't make any sense because we had never experienced it.

I never lost faith in God and seeing loving and kind people always kept me going. Never give up on yourself and humanity and on God.

> Coming from the background I had, if someone talked about love, it just didn't make any sense because we had never experienced it.

*Athiann passed away six months after the recording of this interview. His name has been reprinted to honour his memory.*

# Chapter 10:
# Cheating Death

By B. J., 30-year-old male

My dad is Congolese and my mother is Rwandan. I was eight years old in 1994 when the genocide took place in Rwanda. Our neighbours were killed. I witnessed kids my age being killed; some were my friends. It was an atmosphere of fear. So many people I knew had been killed. After a few months of the killings, a new government came in and many had to flee for safety. We left for neighbouring Congo. To get into Congo, we had to follow the same entry process other refugees had to follow, since my mother was Rwandan. We eventually ended up in my father's homeland in the countryside. In 1996, a civil war started in Congo. Rwandan soldiers started to attack the Rwandan refugees in the Congolese refugee camps because the new Rwandan government feared that the refugees were arming themselves and would stage an attack on the government. We left the camp, got back to Rwanda, and managed to re-establish ourselves in our former home.

## ENDURING MORE WAR

Not long after, in 1998, another civil war broke out close to the border of Congo where we were. Another killing spree started. Soldiers would come to the countryside and kill whoever they found, whether they were children or adults, armed or unarmed. I was quite affected psychologically from experiencing multiple wars and suffered some depression during that time. I came close to death on three separate occasions when we returned to Rwanda. On one occasion, I had gone out with my sister when we came across Rwandan soldiers and rebels. They were fighting about two-hundred metres away. A man standing just a few metres from us was shot and died instantly, right in front of our eyes. My sister and I ran and hid in a lake close by and stayed in the water for two hours until the fighting died down.

*Soldiers would come to the countryside and kill whoever they found, whether they were children or adults*

My second near-death experience happened a little while after. Government soldiers came to our village and killed everyone they could find. Many of the soldiers were looking for revenge for the genocide that had happened to people of their tribe in 1994. They came to our village and started their killing spree at the first house at the entrance to the village. The soldiers broke down doors to whatever house they came to, took everyone outside, and gunned them down. I saw friends get shot in cold blood. I saw the heads of kids explode from bullet shots. It was terrible. We were only saved from death because our house was situated towards the end of the road. Just as the soldiers were going to come to our house, fighting broke out nearby. The soldiers who were supposed to kill us were called to assist where the fighting had broken out, and that's how we made it out alive.

The third incident took place in the same year. I was with my aunty when we came close to where rebel soldiers were. We both ran to hide. My aunty managed to get away, but the rebels found me. They thought I was a government spy since it was common practice for the government to use children to spy on the enemy. The rebels questioned me about my parents and where I came from. None of them had ever heard of my parents, so they decided they would kill me.

Just as they were preparing to kill me, a lady I had never met just showed up and questioned the rebels about what they were about to do. She spoke to me and asked my father's name. When I told her, she knew who he was. She asked me where I was going, and I told her. The lady then spoke to the rebels and convinced them I wasn't a spy. That's how they let me go. One of the rebels even told me, "God saved you today." My mother cried uncontrollably when I told her what had happened.

## LEAVING HOME

In 1999, my older brother who was based in Congo fled to neighbouring Zambia after rebels attacked him there. We did not know that he had moved to Zambia until some years later. Around this same time, conflicts about land started to happen in Rwanda. My family got caught up in it because my father was not Rwandese. Things went from bad to worse, and by the time I was in Grade 12, it just wasn't possible for me to continue living in Rwanda. My brother made contact with us just about then and suggested that I join him in Zambia. Living in Zambia was not perfect, but it was better than both Rwanda and Congo. I was still treated like a foreigner in Zambia, but I was fine with it. It was better than being called a foreigner in the country of my birth.

Living in Zambia was a new chapter in my life. I was not worried about war. My main worry now was just how to put food on the table. I lived one year in the capital city of Zambia, where my brother ran a grocery store. I would sleep in the store at night to keep it safe. During the day, immigration officers would pass through the area to check that all immigrants had the proper documents to be in the country. Later, the checks became frequent and I was afraid of the possibility of being deported back to Rwanda, so I opted to go and stay in the refugee camp to avoid deportation. The refugee camp was near a big forest in the Western Province of Zambia, which allowed the refugees to engage in the business of tree cutting.

## ARRIVING IN CANADA, MY HOME

Not long after, the United Nations High Commissioner for Refugees (UNHCR) came and interviewed me and offered me the opportunity to come to Canada. Within six months, I was on my way. I arrived in Canada in August 2013, in Newfoundland and Labrador. Later, I moved to Alberta.

In the first two years after arriving in Canada, I really struggled with the memories of the things I had gone through. Having friends in Canada really helped. My upbringing also helped me recover. I grew up in a Christian home, and when I got to Alberta, I immediately looked for a church. It took a whole two years of me attending my church before people even noticed who I was, but going there really helped me settle in and recover from the pain of the past. I read a lot and listened to music. Some people with similar backgrounds need to go through counselling, some need just to cry through it or take medications, but for me, my faith was what helped me through.

I have one friend who was with me in Zambia and came to Canada the same time as I did. He got himself into drugs and got a lady pregnant when we came, and he doesn't have a good life. It can be quite difficult to live a normal life after such experiences, but I believe it was God that made the difference for me. I could have ended up just like my friend.

Canada is not heaven, but this has been the best for me. I consider this home now. I don't even imagine going back to my homeland because there is nothing for me to go back to. In the camps, there was no hope for the future. The only thing we hoped for was to see a new day.

*Canada is not heaven, but this has been the best for me.*

I'm thankful to be in Canada. This country is more home to me than the land of my birth.

# Questions and Answers

with Dr. Xavier Mulenga, Psychiatrist

**What is PTSD, and how is it different from other mental issues like depression and anxiety?**

PTSD is post-traumatic stress disorder. In its simplest terms, it is a severe psychological disturbance following a traumatic event. Usually the event is life-threatening, near death, or involves some element of death. It might be something commonly experienced, like a kid witnessing domestic violence between his or her parents, seeing someone die, or working as an emergency rescue worker. Such experiences can be quite traumatic. PTSD can coexist with other mental illnesses. For example, a person could have depression and PTSD, which might show up as a drinking problem. Even just experiencing a racist attack can set off PTSD. In places like the US, some of that racism can turn to death, so just being alive can be almost traumatic in a sense.

The main symptoms of PTSD can be broken down into three levels: re-experiencing the event, hyperarousal avoidance, and emotional numbing.

## Re-experiencing the event

These are people who start getting flashbacks and nightmares. For example, a lady who walks past a place where she was raped could start reliving that experience. People tend to keep that sort of thing to themselves. If, for example, someone who was sexually abused as a child before they came to Canada gets abused again as a university student in Canada, it triggers scars for that event, as well as the old memories. If you didn't know that sexual assault is wrong when you were a child, you might not have felt anything about it at the time. But when someone later points out that sexual assault is wrong, then hate, shame, disappointment, and anger can fester, which can be quite dangerous.

As you get older, you get more aware. **Insight makes you more traumatized**. So a person like that might avoid going to those places that trigger the memories of the trauma. You see something similar in people who come from war-torn countries when they avoid visiting their homelands, even when they have money to make the trip.

## Hyperarousal avoidance

This is usually seen in people you might call "edgy or "jumpy." They seem moody or irritable. The trauma has affected them so much that it has affected their nervous system. It might be the girl at a party who seems uptight or a guy in a racist neighbourhood that knows an attack is imminent. They are tense because their bodies are preparing for an attack. The problem is when you live like that for so long, your body can't tell who's a good person and who's a bad person. Someone who has gone through such trauma may have a difficult time trusting anyone. That affects relationships, how one socializes, works, etc. Sometimes a person may have gone through trauma, but it doesn't seem noticeable. He or she seems to live and function normally but the body always keeps score. All it might take is someone saying, "We are going to have a ten-year college reunion" to have all that trauma return in an instant. In that state, the person will have high-stress hormones, compromised immunity, and such a person becomes sickly and, in some cases, may have suicidal thoughts.

**EMOTIONAL NUMBING**

This where the person becomes an empty person or a shell of herself or himself. Usually, the person will start getting depressive symptoms, become withdrawn, and closed off. This is when other people start noticing that something is wrong and when that person might seek out counselling. By the time a person reaches this point, medications may need to be administered for therapy has to work. Therapy is thirty per cent medication and seventy to eighty per cent behavioural change.

**Can someone who has never directly experienced trauma experience PTSD? Are some people more susceptible to it?**

You can get PTSD vicariously. People such as 911 operators, or people who live with someone who has gone through a traumatic event can experience PTSD. It's rather infectious.

Some factors make it more likely for someone to suffer PTSD. Some of these risk factors may include the following:

- **LOWER EDUCATION AND SOCIAL CLASS.** The lower education one has, the higher the risk of getting PTSD. Immigrants, particularly Blacks and Hispanics, are more vulnerable to PTSD than other racial groups.

- **BEING FEMALE.** Black women, in particular, are the most vulnerable population group, both because of their race and gender. Whenever there is a mental health or drug-addiction issue, they tend to be affected the worst. Women tend not to be believed when they report being sexually abused, and that perpetuates the trauma as well. The other side of this is that women are the ones who usually seek out therapy because they have been socialized to share their problems. So it's not that women are more fragile. Men are just socialized not to talk about their problems. When men with PTSD come for therapy, it's usually quite severe.

- **HAVING PREVIOUS FAMILY HISTORY OF MENTAL ILLNESS.** Issues like depression, anxiety, drug and alcohol addictions, exposure to previous traumatic events, and childhood abuse (sexual, physical and psychological) make one more likely to experience PTSD. Trauma affects the nervous system, so a child who has seen a parent abused has a hyper-aroused nervous system and that leads to burnout and increased susceptibility to PTSD.

Another thing about PTSD is that it tends to recur. It is rare for someone who has been sexually abused once not being abused again later in life. In studies it has been shown that girls tend to first get abused at early ages when they are most vulnerable. Much of it is not violent. It is groomed in by people close to the victim. The victim might be groomed into believing that the more sex she gives, the more gifts she will get. When that person later in life meets men, her brain is so wired from the experiences of the past that she will tend to ignore the reg flags leading to more abuse. The important thing for people who have been through this type of thing is to start putting boundaries around their relationships and using words like "consent" in any relationships they get involved in.

When it comes to sexual abuse, usually people who are close to the victim—family members, uncles, romantic partners— are the ones who inflict the trauma. In the African context, a lot of girls have been through sexual abuse as children, but just didn't call it sexual abuse there and we don't talk about it much.

Some of the protective factors for PTSD are as follows:

- **HIGH INTELLIGENCE.** The more schooling one has, the less likely one is to suffer PTSD because education builds up awareness.

- **HIGHER SOCIAL CLASS.** The higher your social status, the less you worry about things like survival: where food is going to come from or if you will see the next day. Also, people in higher social classes tend to be around similar people, and that can provide positive social support.

- **MALE GENDER.** Men, like those with psychopathic traits, tend to process trauma better, but at the same time, men tend to keep things to themselves, and the trauma can present quite badly when it does come out.

- **GETTING A CHANCE TO VIEW THE BODY OF A DEAD PERSON IN A SAFE ENVIRONMENT.** For example, when training as a medical doctor, you get prepared to face dead bodies and are trained on how to get help if needed.

When you look at the lists, you will find that the risk factors tend to be more present among immigrants, while the protective factors tend to be more common among Caucasians. That's why immigrants are more susceptible to PTSD. Sometimes we think of PTSD among immigrants as something that happens to people coming from war-torn countries, but immigration of any type increases the chances of getting PTSD. Immigrants may struggle to cope with the change to the new culture and often are dealing with trauma that they don't even realize is there.

**What can immigrants do to help make their transitions smoother?**

There are number of things immigrants can do:

1. **EDUCATION AROUND MENTAL ILLNESS.** People should learn about mental health, the symptoms and signs. When people talk about these issues together, they can recognize and support one another when PTSD is being experienced.

2. **SHARING OF RESOURCES (books, workshops, videos, websites).** There are community resources and online resources that can help one know what's going on inside then and how to regulate themselves.

3. **KNOW WHERE TO GO FOR HELP.** This usually involves knowing community mental health centres, church

groups, general practitioners (GPs) or family physicians, psychologists, and psychiatrists. Professionals can provide a framework for the patient to manage PTSD.

**There tends to be skepticism among immigrants about seeking therapy. What value does therapy have and at what point should someone be seeking therapy?**

If you're thinking about therapy, it usually means that you should have been there yesterday. Most people seek out therapy when the situation is beyond their capacity to manage. A person should know and realize how what they are going through is affecting them. If their work, relationships and emotional well-being are being compromised, they probably should be looking at getting therapy. Usually men are less likely to go for therapy and they may come only when things are desperate, like if their marriages are about to end. For men, even something like failing to get a job or promotion can set off PTSD, which then negatively affects their marriages and other relationships. Unfortunately, it is usually the people around you—partners and kids—who get affected when your mental health is not in good shape. If your work and relationships are suffering, or if you are always depressed or crying constantly, it's time to see a therapist.

**BENEFITS OF THERAPY.** There are many benefits of seeking out therapy. Some of them include developing the skills to manage the mental illness or PTSD symptoms, learning coping strategies, being able to see the links between one's behaviours and mental illness, and improved interpersonal relationships. Therapy can help give the skills to know what triggers you and how to work through the anger and other emotions without resorting to negative coping mechanisms like shouting or violence.

**Some claim that the drugs given to help deal with PTSD only make things worse and that many go and do things like commit suicide after taking anti-depressants. What's been your experience as a caregiver, and are there other interventions that people should consider in treating PTSD?**

There is a small percentage of people who have increased suicidal thoughts when first starting anti-depressants. Most doctors prescribing these medications will do a risk assessment to see if those suicidal thoughts are already present. Doctors also usually warn patients that suicidal thoughts are a common side effect of the medications, but that the symptoms usually settle within the first two weeks. The severity of these thoughts depends greatly on the patient, the severity of mental illness, and the availability of social support. This should not deter patients from taking medications, because in the long run they are usually beneficial and great in combination with therapy. Usually just telling patients about the side effects helps relieve the anxiety. Also, most doctors will see a patient weekly or every fortnight when they start anti-depressants just to keep checking up on them. Furthermore, it's always good to give patient 24/7 mental health numbers, information on local mental health community centres, or give them the option that they can present to emergency departments if they feel really suicidal.

**Sometimes, those who have gone through trauma may seem to have coped well during the time in which they experienced the trauma but start to have flashbacks when they are in a place of peace. What causes these episodes to start when things have calmed down?**

When someone is going through the traumatic event (e.g., domestic violence, civil war, abusive parenting), the brain suppresses the body's responses to the extent that people observing may think that someone is coping or managing his or her trauma.

However, when you leave those situations, the flashbacks have a chance to emerge and usually are triggered by a random event. The easiest way to explain this is to talk about soldiers who go to war and during their tour of duty experience a lot of traumatic events, but due to the psychology of the military life, they suppress this trauma. When the soldier returns home and is safe, the trauma may re-emerge. The person may just hear a loud bang in the house and is reminded of bombs going off and friends dying. That moment can reawaken the flashbacks.

**Is this a condition men more than women struggle more with?**

Statistics show that women are impacted more by PTSD, but there might be some bias there, as women are the ones who usually seek out treatment. However, women usually bear the brunt of abusive and trauma against them, for example, sexual assault, domestic violence, gendered homicide, and so forth.

## Is PTSD a first-world problem only?

PTSD is definitely affecting everyone—men, women, and children, Black or white. Statistics show that people in third-world countries do get PTSD, but statistics are usually not documented or reported accordingly. However, in first-world countries, there is an abundance of statistics showing that people from third-world countries have PTSD symptoms or mental illness. Due to the lack of mental health literacy and stigma in many developing countries, mental health illness in many places is just not spoken about.

## Can PTSD disappear by itself, or does it always need some sort of therapy to cure it?

The majority of people don't ever get their PTSD treated but find some way to cope. The general rule of thumb is, the earlier you go for treatment, the less support you will need. If you have recently immigrated from a war-torn country and are screened for PTSD and given support, and told how to access health care supports when unwell, your prognosis is better than another person who seeks help after five to ten years of PTSD symptoms (this is more common in clinical practice).

## Are there things that immigrant communities can do to help notice and help those affected?

Communities need to first educate themselves on what PTSD is. Then they should be given some education on how to spot people with signs of mental illness. These are the first steps, because a lot of communities go head first and try to help with a problem they know very little about. Communities should also help fight stigma by reminding people that mental illness is real and not something that only white people in developed countries get.

Finally, communities should try finding clinicians to hold workshops in a community space/centre on a semi-regular basis. Because, like most things, you probably have to keep reminding people about mental illness and fight the stigma. Religion and church can be very supportive and helpful spaces. It also helps to have key church leaders to have a more robust appreciation of mental illness.

# Part 3:
# The Immigrant Experience
# as an International Student

Of the people who migrate to Canada, a good percentage arrive as students who come with the hope of not only furthering their education but escaping poverty and securing a better future for themselves and their families in Canada. Many come as self-sponsored students who fund their own education or who have their families bearing the burden of their sustenance throughout the duration of their studies. With the average cost of an undergraduate Canadian university education at $32,019 per year in 2020/2021 for international students,[2] the cost of getting a Canadian education is well beyond the reach of most students coming from third-world countries.

For many international students, their aim is to just get a foot into the door. They assume that a way to survive once in Canada will open through scholarships, working while

---

2    "Canadian and International Tuition Fees by Level of Study," Statistics Canada. October 21, 2020, https://www.150.statcan.gc.ca/t1/tbl1/en/tv.action?pid=3710004501. Accessed April 5, 2021.

studying, or through loans. Unfortunately, these assumptions don't always play out as envisioned. Some students end their studies before graduation because of a lack of money, expired study permits, and issues with the law and deportation. The reality of living and studying in Canada can be quite different than the expectations people have before they make the move.

In this chapter, you will hear individuals retell their experiences as international students in Canada: how they dealt with loneliness in Canada's frigid winters, how they survived when they ran out of money, and how they succeeded through it all.

# Chapter 11:
# Getting My Eleven-Year Degree

By N. A., 38-year-old male

I had just finished my studies and was working for my mother and stepfather in Zambia. During that time, my parents decided to leave Zambia for Jamaica to work. They suggested that I consider enrolling for university in Canada, so that I could remain close to where they were and have a chance at securing a better future for myself. I applied to the University of Manitoba and received my acceptance letter within a few months. When the time to leave came, my parents gave me $10,000. I didn't know that that was the last $10,000 they planned to give me.

> My parents gave me $10,000. I didn't know that that was the last $10,000 they planned to give me.

My brother was already in Winnipeg at the time I arrived, so I had someone to come and pick me up from the airport. I lived in a motel for two weeks while looking for a permanent place to stay.

## COPING WITH CULTURE SHOCK

It was April when I arrived and I found it very cold, but I would see people wearing T-shirts outside, which really surprised me. The first time I went to get fast food at A&W, I asked for "chips" and the cashier handed me a small crinkly bag. Feeling a bit insulted, I looked at her and said "I want chips!" to which she responded with surprise. I looked at the menu and realized that what I wanted were known as "fries" in Canada. That was a bit embarrassing. I was giving directions to a friend who had offered to give me a ride home later on and told him to turn right at the "robots," but he had no idea what I was referring to. In Zambia we call traffic lights robots. So even though I had spoken English in Zambia, I found the English spoken here was different.

## DYING DREAMS

My original plan when I got to Canada was to get a computer science degree. I took an introduction to computer programming course in my first semester. My programming instructor taught on the assumption that everyone had a background in computer programming, which I didn't, even though I had taken computer courses back home. I found it difficult to keep up with the material, and I ended up dropping the class. I had been out of school for some years at this point, so not having enough of a foundation in the classes I was taking added to my difficulty in learning the material. My dream of completing a computer science degree died within a few months of my first year of university. I decided I was going to switch to something else.

## FACING FINANCIAL HARDSHIP

When I arrived, my brother was struggling financially, so I used some of my money to pay for both his and my rent, as well our food and other expenses. After paying for our fall tuition fees, the $10,000 my parents had given to me had almost run out. The rules at the time allowed for students to get off-campus work permits, as long as they had been full-time students and passed their courses in the previous semester. But because I had dropped my computer studies class, I did not qualify to apply for the work permit. Thankfully, through some connections, my brother secured jobs for both of us on campus in the food services department. Working there helped us save money for rent and food for the next few months.

By the time we got to the winter semester in January, we had no money to pay for our tuition. International student fees were double that of Canadian students, and the money we made from work was barely enough for rent and food. I contacted my stepdad to let him know about our financial hardship. My parents had sent us to Canada thinking we would find work immediately and take care of our expenses from that point on. But they had never communicated their expectation to us. Thankfully, my stepfather paid for both me and my brother that semester but made it clear that no other financial support would be forthcoming.

I enrolled in my classes, but things were tough. I had to withdraw from one course. As a result, I could not apply for a work permit again since I had lost my full-time student status. I also lost my job on campus, which was also conditional on me maintaining full-time status. We had no money for rent and food. We went back to my parents to ask for help, but they assumed that we were being too lazy to work and just wanted free money.

## FIGHTING FOR SURVIVAL

After that semester ended, my brother found a tree-planting job in Northern Alberta. We bought boots and shovels and set out west for the job. We slept in tents and woke up at 6 a.m. every morning to plant trees for the whole day until evening. Tree planting was very difficult work. The requirements for how many trees to plant in a given area were exact, and if the planting wasn't done perfectly, it all had to be redone. We were paid fifteen cents for every tree we planted in good areas, but in other places we were paid twelve cents per tree. Twenty dollars would be taken from our paycheques each day for food, so nothing was free.

We did not have work permits, so we should not have been working, but we were new to the country and we were in a desperate situation. In the beginning, I planted slowly. I would make about $100 per day, sometimes less. But by the end, I was able to make $200 to $300 a day, enough to pay for my classes for the next semester. The rest of the money went to cover rental arrears that had accumulated because our landlord continued to charge rent even when we had been away. The semester following, I was out of school because I had run out of money. From that time, it was a roller coaster ride. I would be in school one semester and miss the next.

The university, through its International Centre for Students, later started a program where they would give small loans to international students. I applied and was rejected but someone advised me to speak with the director of the International Center for Students. He had lived in Zambia for a few years as a child and had helped many Zambians access the loans. I made an appointment to see him. Things were going well when we met, until he brought up my record. My information showed I had worked off campus when I had gone tree planting, therefore I had breached the conditions of my visa. I confessed. I was quite shocked that he knew about it. He helped me secure the loan nonetheless, and I was very grateful for that. But he told me that my record could hurt me when it came time to renew my study permit.

## EXPIRING STUDY PERMIT

My study permit was soon to expire. The conditions for my visa renewal included having complied with all visa requirements during the study period, maintaining passing grades in all courses, and being in school every semester. I hadn't been in school every semester. Then there was the fact that I had breached the conditions of my visa by working when I did the tree-planting job. I got the loan, made my application, and prayed that the extension would be granted. To my surprise, I got an extension for two more years, but my financial situation remained dire. I had no money and couldn't work.

Even though things were very tough, I never really considered going back to Zambia. That would have meant starting life by myself, but I had nowhere to go and nothing to start from. Additionally, I had already spent a considerable amount of money on my schooling in Canada. Tuition fees had doubled between the time I started school, so all that would have gone to waste had I decided to give up and go back to Zambia. It would have been shameful for me to return with no degree after having spent all that time and money. All those things were weighing heavily on me. Leaving was not an option unless I got deported. I was set on making things work out.

> *It would have been shameful for me to return with no degree after having spent all that time and money.*

When I was in my second last year of school, the law was changed to allow international students to get a work permit, along with their study permit application. The change happened just as my second study permit was about to expire. Around that same time, I started dating my girlfriend (now my wife). She helped me pay for the semester and helped me with the money to apply for my study permit renewal. I was very worried about whether I would get another extension, as I had heard of people who had applied for visa renewals and gotten rejected. Fortunately, I was given an extension for another two years. From that time on, I was able to remain in school every semester. I worked, and my girlfriend's mother (now my mother-in-law) helped by loaning me some money to help me cover my expenses.

## FINDING LOVE

When I was left with one more semester to graduate, my girlfriend and I got married. She got pregnant almost immediately. We had planned to wait until I graduated to have a baby, but things didn't quite work out as planned. The pregnancy was hard on my wife, and I had to rush her to hospital on a few occasions. Between school, work, and hospital visits, things were quite hectic in my last term of school. Thankfully, I made it through my last courses and was able to graduate.

## GRADUATING FROM UNIVERSITY

Graduating was very emotional for me. I cried during the ceremony. It had been eleven long years of trying to get a degree that should have taken me four. Life had been so uncertain during many points of my schooling journey. There were times I felt like I would never get to the end of it. There were times I didn't know where I would get the money for food.

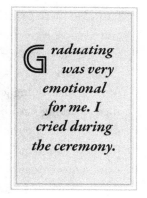

*Graduating was very emotional for me. I cried during the ceremony.*

I believe it is God that saw me through, from my study permit renewals to the times when I had no money for rent and when I almost ran out of food. When I was going through those moments, I would sometimes say, "Why is all this happening to me? I need a breather."

But believing that God was watching over me helped. I used to worry about the future and my plans, where I would get my next meal, and the shame of being deported back to Zambia. But at some point I had to let go and just believe that it would all work out. I realized I did not have control of my life, no matter how much I worried. I was broken. It was in that brokenness I decided to do what I could and leave everything to Him. Worrying didn't help anything. If anything, it hurt my studies when I constantly focused on what wasn't going well. Learning to trust God is what helped me through. If it wasn't for that, I could have easily turned suicidal. In those tough moments you sometimes get tempted to ask, "What's the point of life?"

The most important thing in difficult situations is to have faith. No matter what you are going through, the best thing you can do is leave things in God's hands. I am still not working in my field, despite getting my degree, but I still believe that it will work out. I see people who came to the country as professionals doing jobs they are overqualified for. But I see them working hard because they have a goal to provide for their families and they know things will get better. Take what life gives you, remain humble, and maintain hope that it will work out eventually. I have my degree, and although I am still not quite where I want to be, I am content with what I have and I know it will all work out.

# Chapter 12:
# "Being Yourself," But Not

By L. T., 30-year-old female

When I graduated from high school in Nigeria, there was a national exam we had to write in order to get admission to university. I did mine five times, but because of the corruption in Nigeria, people's exam scores are often sold to other people. So even when you meet the score, you still don't get a place in university unless you pay or bribe someone. After trying for the fifth time, I was exhausted and decided to try looking for a place abroad. I never knew much about Canada, but something just told me to try applying. I applied, I got accepted, and I eventually arrived in Grand Prairie, Alberta, with about fifteen other Nigerians who had also come through the same student recruitment agency.

## COPING WITH CULTURE SHOCK

We were about the only Black people in Grand Prairie when we arrived, and there were many obstacles we had to deal with when we got there. The weather was a big challenge for us, as we had come from a much warmer country, but the people we met were friendly and always smiled at us and invited us into their homes to make us feel at home. The women in our group could not do their hair, and the guys had no place to go to get a haircut; nobody knew how to style our hair. The clothes that were available were not the type we were used to wearing. There were no African foods to eat, so we were stuck with whatever Grand Prairie had. For example, to make our traditional soup back home, we usually would use palm oil to help give the soup its red colour, but it was not available in Grand Prairie. We had to improvise to make things work.

Another challenge I faced was in class with my instructors. I had studied in English in Nigeria, but it was so hard to understand my Canadian instructors. Their English was different from what I was used to. I had to have a hundred percent concentration on the lecture the whole time, otherwise I'd not catch a word of what was being taught. Sometimes I'd just laugh when the instructor said something funny, not because I understood the joke but I just wanted to fit in. I found the curriculum taught in Canada to be challenging.

> Sometimes I'd just laugh when the instructor said something funny, not because I understood the joke but I just wanted to fit in.

I was a science student in high school in Nigeria. I had done classes in biology, chemistry, and physics and really enjoyed them. I decided I would do petroleum engineering in university, but I now found sciences very challenging. For example, in chemistry, we didn't have actual equipment in our laboratories in Nigeria, but in Canada you saw the real thing. If the instructor said hydrogen plus oxygen gives you water, you actually saw those chemical reactions happen right in front of you. But strangely, it was actually all quite confusing. It was a different chemistry from what I had learned. Physics was different from the physics I had known in Nigeria, too. I used to love mathematics, but now I was struggling with it. The grading scheme was also very different. In Nigeria, if you scored seventy per cent you would be considered an A student, but here it wasn't the same.

Outside that, we came in at the time when you could not work off-campus. Being in a small city, finding work on-campus was very difficult because it was a small campus and we had no Canadian work experience. Out of the fifteen of us, only two were able to find work on-campus, but the rest of us struggled. Money was an issue for most of us. When our parents needed to send us money, they had to change the money from Naira to US dollars first, then have it changed to Canadian dollars, so our parents started to have financial difficulties. Before coming, we assumed the US and Canadian dollar were the same. Whenever I wanted to buy food or clothes, I would always do a conversion to compare what a similar item would cost in Nigeria. Usually things seemed a lot more expensive here, comparatively, so I would struggle to even buy food.

I don't even know how I survived all that when I think about it now. One time, I was forced to do a cleaning job with a lady because I was getting desperate for money. She was paying me under the table because I could not get a job off-campus.

Some of the ladies in our group encountered challenges with their health. They would miss their menstrual periods for two or three months, and whenever they went to the doctor for a checkup, they were always told the same thing: the weather change was affecting the hormones in their bodies.

## MOVING WEST

After finishing my one-year university transfer program in Grand Prairie, I decided to move to Winnipeg to attend the University of Manitoba. It was the cheapest university for international students at the time, and admission was fairly easy to get. I had given up on my petroleum engineering dreams and decided to do an economics degree instead.

Winnipeg was a much bigger city and more diverse, so it was a little easier to fit in. We tried to do the things that the locals did. For instance, many Canadian students would leave their rooms unlocked, which was completely unthinkable in Nigeria. But we didn't want to seem stuck up so we also started to leave our doors open, even when we were not in our rooms. Unfortunately, we had an incident where some laptops and money went missing, so that was a big lesson to learn.

## EXPERIENCING A DIFFERENT CULTURE SHOCK

It was difficult for me to find work after graduating. At the time I graduated, the rules were that for you to keep your work permit and apply for permanent residence, you needed to find a job related to your field of studies. I majored in economics and minored in business management, so finding work in that field was a challenge. When I did get into the working world, I was surprised to see that many people holding high positions didn't even have a degree. That was discouraging because I had spent all this money to get a degree, and it seemed like it wasn't even that important at the end of it all. Experience seemed to count more than education. I did not know how to compete in the working world.

> **I** had spent all this money to get a degree, and it seemed like it wasn't even that important at the end of it all.

Then there were corporate politics, which really surprised me. I have struggled to stay in my jobs because I don't know how to play the game. I feel like I can't be myself at work. Whenever I am myself, people don't like it and kick me out of the job. It's very frustrating. They say we should be ourselves but when we are, it causes conflict. One time at a certain company, I noticed a colleague was crying. I reached out to her to help because I could not watch her just cry, but I got reprimanded for it. I was told I had to be professional and that next time I should just reach out to the supervisor and report the situation.

Recently, I quit another job with an internet-service provider around the time the COVID-19 pandemic started. There was so much pressure at work. We were told we had to meet our targets, despite the disruption caused by the pandemic. I called the supervisor out and told him that it was unreasonable to expect so much out of us considering the turmoil going on. All they seemed to care about was their numbers. I told him I needed to go on stress leave and didn't want to be bothered about work. I found them heartless. Our hours had been reduced, and they were still putting pressure on us to meet their numbers. I decided I couldn't work there and quit my job. Before the COVID-19 pandemic started, the company would talk about how much they cared for their employees, but when they had a chance to prove it, they showed that they really didn't care as much as they claimed.

I really struggle with what seems to me as a fake life here. I was watching the news one evening during the pandemic and it mentioned how the government wanted immigrants to work in the hospitals to help manage the pandemic. They said that there was no longer a need for immigrants to write the exam to allow them to practice, and that some fees that would usually be charged were going to be waived. It upset me that all the while before the pandemic, there had been all these requirements that people had to meet to allow them to practice, but when there was a crisis, all of the sudden, none of the rules and requirements mattered. It's like the laws are not really made to favour those that need the help.

I feel the pandemic has exposed a lot of weaknesses in the systems we have been told to trust. The rules don't seem to be there to benefit immigrants. People go through long processes to get their credentials certified from their home countries, only to be denied the opportunity to practice when they get here. In 2006, I met a Nigerian doctor who owned a practice in Nigeria. He applied and received his permanent residence and sold everything to come to Canada. When he arrived, he could not practice as a doctor and had to work as a health-care aid. He regrets that he came but he is stuck because he closed everything down in Nigeria to make the move to Canada. One thing the government can do is put such people in a class where they can work maybe as nurses while they get Canadian experience. It's painful when people have to start at the bottom when they come to Canada.

When you look at the educational system, they gave us loans once we became permanent residents, but at the end of the day, you can't get a job and you are on the hook for the money. I took $16,000 for a two-year program after university and I can't find a job. I'm now forgetting what I learned and yet I have to pay back all that money.

It has been hard to settle in these workplaces, and I feel I can't be who I am there. I would like to start my own business, but I'm also considering a return to Nigeria one day soon. We will see what the future holds.

# Chapter 13:
# Finding Success Through Disappointment

By O. S., 32-year-old female

I come from Nigeria. My original plan was to study in the United States, but I was denied a visa, so Canada was the next country in line for me. Soon after I applied to Canada, I got my visa to study and arrived alone in St John, New Brunswick, in the winter of 2009. The school was closed at the time, but a local lady picked me up from the airport and volunteered to let me stay in her house.

## FINDING MYSELF

I spent my first four months almost never going outside. It was cold, and I was very homesick during that time. Human interaction seemed very limited in St John. Everyone just minded their own business, so it was difficult to get to know people. In my lectures, I could barely understand what was being

> In my lectures, I could barely understand what was being said, even though I spoke English.

said, even though I spoke English. I found the way English is spoken in the Maritimes very challenging to understand, so there was a communication barrier due to language and the different teaching style that I found in Canada.

I eventually made friends, and that helped me settle in quickly. I got involved on campus with the multicultural society and the African society, where I and got elected as vice president. I volunteered in the International Student's Society doing airport pickups and helping new students settle in and make friends. I made sure to occupy myself with activity, and that helped my integration into society.

Most international students who came to the Maritimes were quite disciplined. It was the students that settled in bigger cities like Toronto and Montreal, who often had issues with drinking and partying. Those who came to a small place like St Johns were really serious about the reason they came. There were, however, some unfortunate incidents involving international students sometime later, when more international students started to come in. There was one case where a male international student went to a club and took a drunk girl back to his room. After the encounter, the lady filed assault charges and he was arrested and deported. This student was about to be granted his permanent residence but because of that incident, he lost everything. Some behaviours that would have gone unpunished in a place like Nigeria, such as flirting or passing certain compliments, can be considered harassment in Canada. Some international students learned that lesson the hard way when they got themselves into trouble.

## ENTERING THE WORKPLACE

Transitioning to the workplace was almost harder than the initial settling in. As international students, many of us had the belief that as soon as we graduated it would be easy to find work, especially from a technical field like engineering. I moved to Alberta with big dreams of getting a job quickly and making lots of money with a big oil and gas company. Those expectations were soon crushed by the harsh realities of the working environment.

> *Many of us had the belief that as soon as we graduated it would be easy to find work*

I started to see the culture in a different light. Some graduates came to Alberta and were making minimum wage. I ended up in a technical sales role and was doing quite well, despite the unfriendly environment which was heavily male-dominated. The government has made in-roads supporting women in trades, but a lot more can be done. I was the only woman, the only Black person, and I was the youngest worker there. A lot of clients were not comfortable with my presence and thought I was not deserving of my position. If I asked for help to lift something they would respond by saying, "Well, women want equality; why can't you lift it?" However, my manager was very supportive. Unfortunately, he quit after a while, and my new manager was not as supportive as my previous one had been.

In 2015 when the recession hit, I was laid off even though our company was doing well. The manager brought in another person and replaced me, so I felt that the new management didn't want me around. Companies by law are made to diversify the selection of their employees, so sometimes they take in minorities just to be viewed as equal-opportunity employers as people will frown upon them if they are not seen to be hiring minorities. I felt like I was just being used as a statistic and when they felt they didn't need me anymore, they got rid of me.

I saw minority employees with experience in engineering work being managed by people who didn't even finish high school and frustrating their employees who tried to explain technical drawings or provide rationale for making certain decisions. When it comes to hiring decisions, I understand that it's not just an issue of colour. People want to hire people who they can relate to and who they share similar interests with. In industry, a lot of people's friends are their work colleagues. Many Africans, on the other hand, tend to prefer to keep their work life and home lives separate. Among Canadians, if they can't see you as a friend, it's harder for them to hire you.

Most people spend the majority of their lives at work. I have seen situations where the popular guy at work doesn't do his job properly but never gets fired. A friend of mine got laid off from a company, but another guy more junior than him remained. This junior guy was the one always bringing coffee and doughnuts for the office and attending all company social events. My advice to minority professionals is to be open. Go curling, learn how to skate, and get more involved instead of restricting yourself to your community.

## BOUNCING BACK

I started looking for other work, but all the jobs I got were not stable, and I kept getting laid off. In one job, a new employee was brought to me to train. I was laid off soon after. That sort of thing became normal.

Right now, I am running my own immigration consulting business, and I think my experiences have been a blessing in disguise. I realize that for me to thrive in a foreign land I need to have my own business because companies will always prioritize their own people. In many companies, you are just a number. I set up my business in Canada with a branch in Nigeria, which has expanded and developed partnerships with companies in South Africa, Tanzania, Namibia, and Zambia. My company helps people in these countries come to Canada by setting them up with childcare with jobs in Canada.

Chinese or Indian immigrants have thrived because they have set themselves up well. I feel Black people need to be more business-focused. The issue is that most African parents celebrate their child when he or she says, "I got a job as a manager" but when that child says "Dad, Mom, I want to start a business," it doesn't excite them. I run a business and I'm making more than I did when I was working for someone and I have more freedom and more independence to travel. But I still have some family members ask me, "When are you going back to work?" We need to get out of that mindset. It's good to have a job. There is nothing wrong with that, but it is always good to do something on the side that will give you gratification. I am very involved in the refugee community, helping those in hiding. I do financial empowerment for Africans, and I give seminars on how to start a business.

## Offering Advice to Young Immigrants

> *A lot of people come here and get distracted by so many things such as social media and wanting to show off and trying to impress other people.*

Stay focused and have a clear objective. A lot of people come here and get distracted by so many things such as social media and wanting to show off and trying to impress other people. The best way to succeed is to maintain focus, have a clear objective, and hang around the right circles. The Minister of Justice in Alberta is a Nigerian man, and we have another who just joined the law chambers. These are people who are known in the community for being focused. They are not out there gossiping; they are passionate about helping people. A lot of people prioritize the wrong things and spend time on non-productive things. Things are not as rosy here as they may look from our home countries, so people should do as much research as they can and make sure they are making an informed choice before they decide to come.

# Chapter 14:
# Making My New Home

By B. Z., 31-year-old female

I came to Canada from Zimbabwe in 2007 for university. I was originally going to go to South Africa for my studies since I had gotten a place at one of the universities there. I had a lot of family in South Africa, but I wanted to be in a place by myself and discover who I am, so I chose Canada because I wanted to be away from the familiar. There was a student recruiting agency in Zimbabwe, which helped with putting applications in to Canadian universities. The agency wasn't very good. They over-promised and under-delivered. They promised things like access to scholarships, an airport pickup, and other things once I arrived in Canada, but none of that happened.

> I chose Canada because I wanted to be away from the familiar.

Even though I was excited about coming to Canada, I was nervous at the same time. Everything was going to be new. I was nervous about settling in, but I wasn't nervous about leaving my family because I knew I would see them over most school holidays. I chose to study at the University of Manitoba, because the program I wanted to take was priced lower than the same program at other Canadian universities.

## HEADING TO WINNIPEG

While making my application to study in Canada, I met someone else who also happened to be planning to attend the University of Manitoba. We were to arrive in the country on the same day, so we planned to meet at the Winnipeg International airport once we arrived. But my flight got delayed. By the time I arrived, the other person had already gone, so I ended finding my way to the university alone. The road leading out from the airport was in rough shape, and I remember thinking to myself, *Is this really Canada?* I did not expect to see roads in Canada as bad as the ones I had left in Africa. That was my first impression. Before I came, I'd imagine Canada having skyscrapers and perfect roads, but Winnipeg did not look like that. I was a little disappointed, to be honest. Things got better, though.

When I got on campus, I located my residence, got my room and keys, and tried to find the friend I had met while in Zimbabwe. I did not know any other person in Canada. I met a friend from South Korea. She was God sent. She was a very nice person and really helped me out. In the residence, we had no option but to eat food from the cafeteria. It was a requirement to pay for the campus food plan to show that one had enough money to live in Canada. After a year on campus residence, I moved and rented an apartment.

I did quite well in my first year of university, but I started to struggle a bit with school a little later into my studies. I wanted to be an actuarial scientist, but my grades were just not quite high enough. I was paying international student fees, which at the time were double the amount locals paid, so I couldn't afford to waste time or money. I switched over into the finance program, which was a close alternative. In the end, I graduated with a degree in finance and international business.

I was lucky not to struggle with money issues during my time of study. My parents paid for everything. I worked a little while studying, but it was mostly for pocket money. Later, I started to pay for my living as well. I really don't know how my parents managed it, because it was a lot of money.

## LOSING MY FATHER

When I was graduating, my family could not come to my ceremony. My dad was very sick at the time. My graduation ceremony was in June and my dad passed away in July. It was tough not having my family there, but I had made many friends over the years who came out to support me. The university live-streamed the event, so my family were able to celebrate with me even though they were not physically present.

## MAKING WINNIPEG MY HOME

Getting permanent residency when I graduated was straightforward and perhaps easier than it is today. All you had to do was work for the same employer for at least six months, and that made you eligible to apply. Things seem harder now. I had no intentions of staying in Canada permanently, but things in my home country have become so bad so my parents advised me to stick it out. My original intention was to return to Zimbabwe after graduating. I'd like to move back some day, but for now I am staying in Canada.

I'm happy with the way my life has progressed, and I thank God for how my life has turned out.

I believe things always eventually work out no matter what season you are in. I've always wanted to leave Winnipeg from the day I arrived, but it has never happened. I've accepted this is now home for me. I look back and say, "It's not so bad after all." I've been able to buy my own home, and that's only because the cost of living here is low compared to bigger cities in Canada. There are positive things in every situation.

> I've always wanted to leave Winnipeg from the day I arrived, but it has never happened.

# Chapter 15:
# Accepting Vulnerability

By F. M., 33-year-old female

I live in Manitoba, Canada, but originally come from Zambia. I came to Canada to study, but my original plan was to go to South Africa because I wanted to remain in close proximity to my family. My family has always been important to me, and I could not imagine needing to take three or four plane rides whenever I wanted to see them. I ended up choosing the University of Manitoba in Winnipeg because the university had been conducting a campaign in Zambia to attract people to study. Schools from the United States, the United Kingdom, and Australia were also recruiting students, but the University of Manitoba had the cheapest fees, so it made sense to choose Winnipeg. I was only seventeen at the time, and my brother was already a student in Winnipeg. That, combined with lower fees and their well-reputed architecture program, attracted me to Winnipeg.

## SETTLING IN

It made a big difference that my brother was already in Canada when I arrived. Everything was in place for me, from accommodation to school arrangements. I remember taking a walk one day in my early days and saying hi to a lady I met along the way. The lady smiled back and asked me where I was from. I told her I was from Zambia and her next question was, "How long have you been here?" I told her I had been in the country for a few weeks and her response to me was, "Your English is so good." That surprised me a little because I had done all my schooling in English.

I also found it strange how quiet the people were. While in Zambia, I had lived in an apartment block, and it was always noisy there. But in Canada, apartment buildings were so quiet. Nobody spoke to each other; everybody got into their apartments and closed their doors behind them. Nobody knew anybody. It felt like Canada was cold, not just with the weather but also with the people. My first impressions changed after a while. People in Canada are friendly, but it does take some effort to befriend them, whereas back home, making friends would happen effortlessly.

## BEING ALONE AND LONELY

When it came to my academics, I didn't have real problems adjusting to the Canadian learning environment. There were quite a number of immigrants in all my classes, which made settling in easier. I found instructors to be warm and welcoming, but it was hard to make friends in class, partly because the small talk in Canada is different from back home. The things that Caucasians casually talk about and the things that immigrants talk about are different, so I'd feel left out of conversation, even though I spoke good English. Because of that, I did not have any friends in the first few months of my classes.

I was on the phone with my family all the time in those first few months because I was very lonely and knew nobody, except my brother. It helped that I went to church. The people there would invite me over to their homes to visit and share a meal, so that really helped. Despite all that, I did well in school, probably because I had nothing else to do but study. I had very few interests in common with most students because I wasn't into partying or clubbing.

In my classes, I was very reserved and afraid of being uncomfortable and vulnerable. Where I come from, you would never call an instructor by their first name or challenge them in any way as that would be seen as disrespect. But in Canada, if you had to move along, you had to be seen as assertive and vocal, and I didn't have that in me. In the faculty of architecture in which I was enrolled, there were many tight cliques, and I would stay away from joining them in part because I didn't was to look dumb in front of my peers. Sometimes I would stand near a group of people just to listen and get a sense of the types of things they talked about, because nothing I talked about seemed interesting to anyone. Because of that and my fear of vulnerability, I stayed away from networking events, and I lost out on many opportunities when the time to find work came.

> Where I come from, you would never call an instructor by their first name or challenge them in any way as that would be seen as disrespect.

## GROWING CONFIDENT

Towards the end of my undergraduate degree, one or two of my instructors made the effort to invest in me personally and drew out my potential. They helped me become more confident, and by the time I was leaving school, I believed in my ability to present and defend my ideas. By the time I got into the workforce, I was able to stand up for myself and advocate for others.

## SEARCHING FOR A JOB

When I finished school, I thought I just needed to get certified as an architect in order to practice, but that's not how things worked. I realized only after that I needed a master's degree. Doing a master's was challenging because I also wanted to get my permanent residency. In order to do that, I had to have a job, so I couldn't be picky. Then there was the fact that I had ignored networking events while a student, which made it even harder to find work in my field. I had to decide between taking the time to look for work in my field or getting any job I could find to get the process for my permanent residence going. Around that time, my husband had to leave Canada, and that also added to the challenge of getting my permanent resident status. In the end, I decided to take a job as a secretary with the Province of Manitoba. Several people had told me I would never get a government job without my permanent resident status, but I decided to apply and got the job.

## LIVING WITHOUT MY HUSBAND

Having my husband leave the country set me back a little because I had wanted to do my master's degree. I had grown up with my mind set on going to school, getting work, then getting married—in that order. Dealing with my husband's immigration issues felt like a setback. My plan had been to work for a year and save money for my graduate studies or maybe for a house. But because my husband was back in Africa, I had to work and help support him, so there were a lot of expenses I had to deal with that I had not anticipated. It did not help that my parents were not supportive of my marriage because they knew that I was probably giving my husband support. That created tension among us.

On the other hand, many good things happened during that period. I always had dreams and plans, and those stayed in my head. I never gave up on my plan to go to school, and knew I was going to do my master's degree as soon as my husband was back. I knew how to keep moving on, so I kept the next steps in mind despite everything that was going on. I never really stopped to feel bad about things because I could see the end. The constant back and forth with Canadian immigration was draining, but having my brother in the US and my husband's family within Canada really helped. I saw them as often as was possible, and that helped me cope.

> I never really stopped to feel bad about things because I could see the end.

## LISTENING TO A MOTHER'S WISDOM

My mother is a very confident woman, and she always told me, "Nobody can make you sad without your consent." I have always kept that at the back of my mind. I also believe in God, and that has helped me in moments of anxiety. Those things have helped me get over setbacks fairly easily. I have never been attached to any particular dream, and when things don't work out, I tend to believe that it wasn't God's will for them to happen. I don't dwell on "Why?" too much. My mother always instilled in me and my siblings that we have a role to advocate for others and to stand up for what we believe in. She raised us to be confident, yet humble. She told us that we could do whatever we wanted to do. Sometimes, I feel that I have to be different things to different people here. At work, I feel it's important that people know that I am African, and that I am proud of it. But there are certain things that we would never do in our culture, like challenge our boss. Yet, in Canada, that's the way you get ahead. You need to have your voice heard, which is very un-African.

Things other people see as a drawback, instead are an advantage for me. I am a Black woman, and I see that as a good thing. Companies want diversity, so I see that as an opportunity to get hired. I have always had the attitude to use my peculiarity to my advantage.

> In many ways, we immigrants are helping to build a better Canada.

In many ways, we immigrants are helping to build a better Canada. We come with a different culture and a different way of thinking about problems, so speaking up and being heard helps build up this society. This is our home as well. Everyone, including the Caucasians, at one point migrated to this land, so we should not feel like we do not belong here.

## BALANCING WORK, FAMILY, AND CAREER

I am grateful that I have had my time to go after my career. I enjoyed school. I got a job that I really liked, but I feel that motherhood is my focus at this point in my life. I don't even miss my job any more. I have considered not returning to work or maybe changing my career and doing something that allows me to work from home. But after chasing after a career for so long, I am reminded, at the end of the day, that family is what really matters. I have to figure out what that looks like for me.

## OFFERING WORDS OF SUPPORT

It's important to have good people around you and not waste time with people who do not add value to your life. Just two or three people invested in you will make a big difference. Getting into a faith-based community has also worked for me. I would advise people to keep their heads up and not have the attitude of shying away and feeling like you don't belong. That doesn't do anything for us. We are here, and we have to give our best. Whatever you find yourself doing, do it well, and don't worry about being looked at as different. Don't let your colour or accent stop you from speaking up. Canada is diverse, so use it to your advantage. Sometimes we blame racism for our inability to get ahead. But you can always turn that around. There are opportunities that exist here specifically for women, minorities,

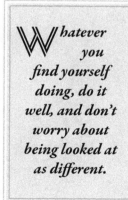

*Whatever you find yourself doing, do it well, and don't worry about being looked at as different.*

and other underrepresented communities. Use those to your advantage. I always feared being vulnerable or to look foolish, but you can only grow when you allow yourself to be vulnerable and make mistakes.

# Chapter 16:
# Breaking Barriers
By N. Y., 39-year-old female

I t was 1995 when my mother came to Canada from Jamaica to be with my oldest sister. She eventually decided to stay in Canada and never returned. I had graduated and was working in Jamaica and wanted to visit Canada to see my family. I went to the embassy to get a visa and my application was denied four times. After the fourth denial, I was almost at the point of giving up ever coming to Canada. I knew the only way I was going to come to Canada was if my mother sponsored me. That's what she did, but the visa was denied yet again. I figured that the only way that was left for me to come to Canada was if I came in as a full-time student, so I gave up my job in Jamaica and came to Canada with the help of my mother.

## RETURNING TO SCHOOL

I knew that for me to be successful in Canada, I had to go back to school. There was no getting around it. I realized early that for an immigrant to succeed and to stand out and be different, you had to get Canadian education. I ended up going to school full-time for seven years. I did a diploma and bachelor's degree, so that I would be equipped when I entered the working world.

One thing I quickly realized was that people related differently in Canada. I found that even though one might speak the same words, meanings can be quite different. I was in college and sitting in an accounting class when the professor asked a question. In Jamaica, you would raise your hand and snap your fingers if you know the answer to a question. So I raised my hand and snapped my fingers like I was used to back home and the instructor said, "Who do you think you are snapping your fingers at? Do I look like a dog?" I was clueless about why the instructor reacted the way she did. To me, I was snapping my fingers because I knew the answer. I failed that class because I shut down emotionally and couldn't come back to myself for the rest of the semester.

> *I found that even though one might speak the same words, meanings can be quite different.*

## MOVING FROM MANITOBA TO SASKATCHEWAN

I realized early on that there wasn't a big emphasis on having credentials in the Canadian work environment, which was different from back home where credentials meant everything.

When I finished university, I moved to Saskatchewan from Manitoba. The provincial government in Saskatchewan had a tax incentive program for students, so that made it attractive to move.

Being in a small town in Saskatchewan had its challenges for a minority. Once, I went to Block Busters to get something and the clerk did not want to touch my hand as he was giving me my change. He just dropped it on the counter for me to collect. That happened about three times.

I worked in banking as a teller, and there would be people who would refuse to be served by me. They would wait forever for another teller to be free rather than come to me. I'm not entirely sure what was behind that behaviour. Maybe it's that people were not used to people like me. My family was only one of two Black families in town, so maybe some people were not used to having people like us around; perhaps there was some racism there. I am more mature about such things now. They just don't affect me. If someone doesn't want to relate to me, I just leave them alone. If I see someone being racist, I try to educate them. At the time when I came to Canada, there were few Black people, even in big cities like Winnipeg, but things have changed a bit since. I feel being confident in yourself helps one get through these things. I have educated myself, so when people do such things, it just doesn't bother me because I know who I am.

> If someone doesn't want to relate to me, I just leave them alone.

## CHALLENGING EXPERIENCES

The most difficult experience I've had being in Canada was deciding to sponsor my husband to join me in Canada and finding out that he married me just to get to Canada. That was hard to get past. My spirituality helped me in a big part, and being six hours away from where he lived helped me as well.

## MOVING BEYOND BARRIERS

I'm proud of completing university. My daughter came as a result of my ex-husband wanting to prevent me from finishing school. It was his way of trying to sabotage my career and future. I remember I went to school with her right up to my last month of pregnancy. I went to school the whole week after I gave birth to my daughter, aside from the one day following the delivery, and I never missed another day until my graduation. I am proud that I persisted and finished my degree. I'm also proud of completing my master's degree. I had just had my second child at the time and was able to complete that with two kids. Barriers motivate me. I use them to motivate myself to prove to myself that I can do whatever I want to do.

# Questions and Answers

with Dr. Madalitso Chundu, MD

**Many immigrants have challenges settling into the system when they come to Canada as young adults. What strategies have you found helpful?**

The challenge is not having someone ahead of you to tell you what strategies locals use to get through, so you have to make your own mistakes and learn the hard way. My advice for newcomers is to access whatever resources are available to you. Don't try to rewrite the rules or carve out your own path. You will set yourself up for failure if you try to figure it out for yourself.

From my own academic experience, I found high school in Canada easier than I did in Africa. The teachers in Canada were much more dedicated to their students than African teachers were. I felt that teachers were very willing to give of their time to me. In university, realizing how to understand the systems necessary to succeed was what I found challenging. For example, in order to be a pre-med student, you had to have a specific number of pre-med courses and there's a specific way to take them. Having even a single course with a B grade could hurt you when trying to get into medicine. You never took organic chemistry in a regular session because it was a known GPA buster. You had to take it in the summer by itself in the first or second year. You would never take physics, biology, and chemistry together in order to keep your GPA up. But those were things I don't know, and I learned them the hard way. I wish there could have been someone to guide me.

Being successful is not just about academics. Immigrants are completely capable of performing as well as anyone else academically, but it's the psychosocial element that can be hard for new immigrants. My advice for newcomers is to immediately find a mentor who approximates where you want to be. That's how even native-born North Americans get ahead. They are a few steps ahead simply because they have an uncle or cousin that's already travelled the path they are headed. Most immigrants don't have that, and that's why mentorship matters. A mentor will help you see things you might never find out by yourself.

Sometimes there are things stacked against you that you don't even realize. I work with African-American doctors and they tend to see some things much more readily than African immigrants. Where I might blame myself for failure, an African-American doctor is much more likely to say that the system is bent against us so the mindset is one that says you have to work hard to beat the system. It seems paranoid, but at the same time it gives you the mental strength to take on the difficult aspects of success in any field.

Sometimes as immigrants, we have to unlearn some of what we know about how to deal with life and with problems. In an African home, you are taught to be humble and differential to other people. It's almost rude to be assertive, especially to people who are authority. It's something that was very diffi-cult for me to unlearn. The attitude of being quiet or humble often made my professors not trust me or think that I was less capable of my colleagues who were more up front. As medical students, we would be assigned to work in teams and be provided with a list of patients we would be responsible for. Usually the resident doctor would assign that list to the person who they thought showed the most responsibility.

My non-immigrant friends would naturally know the dynam-ics at play and would very quickly position themselves as the person in charge by stepping up to the plate and not apologiz-ing for it. For me, even when I recognized the dynamics, it didn't come instinctively to step up the way my local friends did. I found I was consistently looked over and, as a result, my evaluations suffered. My supervisors would think I was not as knowledgeable about things, yet I had been working as hard or even harder than my colleagues. Being able to take control of a situation and confidently move into a circumstance is something we generally don't have in our culture, but is the basis in which promotion happens here.

**How can communication between parents and their young adult children be improved?**

There are challenges that young people face that their parents, in most cases, will not face. Parents who come to Canada when they are older are usually just looking to get into the workforce and make enough for their families to survive. Young people have the luxury of being able to choose things that they find fulfilling. Where parents become useful is in being able to affirm their kids. Parents need to be able to tell their children how proud they are of them and that they love them. In many African or immigrant cultures, if you are in trouble at school with your teacher, for example, you are also in trouble with your parents. If you fail an exam, then it must be because something is wrong with you and the teachers did not contribute anything to your failure.

It's important, especially in this culture, for parents to affirm their kids even more than they would have done in their home countries, because you don't get that from anyone else here. If a child doesn't end up as a doctor or engineer, parents sometimes make it seem almost as if the child has brought shame to the family. Yet the parents need to be the child's biggest cheerleaders. When a parent is not proud of his or her child, the child feels it, even when a parent tries not to talk about.

A parent should be okay with letting children decide for themselves. Sometimes parents feel that because they have sacrificed for the sake of the child, that the child needs to follow the template the parent has laid out for the child's life. That sometimes leads to frustration for both. When a child gets out into the world, all the negative voices are amplified. Nobody cheers for you; there are no prizes for second-place finishers. If you fail, people just look at you and walk away. A person often does not have a strong basis on which to be confident outside the affirmation that parents give, and if the parent doesn't give it, that child goes elsewhere to find it.

**How does an immigrant overcome obstacles to finding success in North America?**

For someone that grew up in North America, things like being assertive, managing time effectively, or sticking to a schedule are things that are built into the culture. Whereas for someone who was brought up in Africa, for example, those are things that have to be learned when we settle here. They are not emphasized or taught in our educational systems and are not a big part of our culture. I would recommend first of all recognize that in whatever you do, you should aim to be open to learning and always seek to provide value to others. Sometimes the mindset we have as immigrants is to just come in and get a secure stable job so that we can feed our families. Very few African immigrants view this as a place where they can thrive and climb to being a mayor or member of Parliament, for example. Very few come in with a long-term plan. Part of that is the mindset of just wanting to provide for one's own family and maybe return "home" at some point in the future.

In order to be able to lead, you have to provide value to other people outside yourself and your family. As you do that, people start to recognize you for it. In many places we come from, you are handpicked for promotion or for increased responsibility, but in this culture you have to be the one to initiate your promotion. You have to have the mindset that says, "I'm not here to benefit myself," and go in to serve others. You might not enjoy their social events or making small talk, but you need to develop the mindset that you are not going for yourself but for the benefit of others. If you do that consistently, people see it and they become comfortable giving you responsibility.

When you do get into leadership, you will face challenges. You will find people who are sometimes more eloquent than you are. There are some who just want to fight you, don't want to be told anything, and try to embarrass you, so you have to do what you are good at and do it well. The people born here tend to be good at playing the long game. They can get into the most junior positions and stay five or ten years and work themselves up the ladder. That's a different mindset from the typical African. There tends to be a sense of entitlement that comes with us when we graduate with a university degree. We often believe we deserve a management position in a company on day one, but you have to be ready to take the time that is needed to climb the ladder over time to succeed in this culture.

Volunteerism is something more of us have to consider. In developing countries, the societies tend to be hierarchical and authoritarian. Someone who runs a business will not be seen sweeping the floor, for example. We don't have the spirit of servant leadership. In this society the boss tends to be the hardest worker. If his or her employees work forty hours, he will put in sixty, and it can be quite the challenge for many of us who have not grown up in that sort of service environment.

**What would your advice be to young adults who want to make it in this environment but not lose themselves in the process?**

It would be helpful for immigrants to adopt a growth mindset. Some research carried out by Angela Duckworth and Carol Dweck studied two groups of kids. One group of kids are identified early as very highly talented but ended up unsuccessful over the long-term. The other group, despite having lower aptitudes, ended up successful as grown-ups. They studied what it was about the two groups that made the difference and they identified what they called a growth mindset. A person with a growth mindset is one who views everything in life as possible to achieve with hard work. The other side is people who have a fixed mindset—people who will try one thing and move onto the next when they feel it's not working out for them. A person with a growth mindset will say, "I can't do it yet" when they come across something difficult. They believe that everything is achievable. They believe that with hard work they can accomplish anything. My encouragement to young adults is that they develop a growth mindset. Do not place limits on yourself and you can and will do great things.

# Part 4:
# The Immigrant Experience and Marriage

When couples migrate to Canada, they often look for jobs that can get them the most money in the quickest time. Women typically find themselves with more and better options, in part because many of jobs that are easily available to newcomers are found in the healthcare field, which is largely female dominated. A good example of this is the healthcare aide profession—a high-in-demand profession with abundant work, decent wages, overtime, and shift premiums. Course can be taken in under eight months for a very reasonable cost in most Canadian provinces.[3]

Many immigrant women join this profession and are quickly able to settle into Canadian society. Immigrant men, on the other hand, might come from places where such work may be considered "women's professions." They will avoid such work in preference for jobs similar to what they did before coming

---

3  Health Care Aide Courses, Program and Training, CDI College, Manitoba. https://www.cdicollege.ca/manitoba/programs-and-courses/healthcare/health-care-aide/. Accessed April 5, 2021.

to Canada. Unfortunately, this is often met with frustration when they find out that they have to upskill or re-skill in order to be employable in their former professions.

Consequently, men find themselves with limited options for work that carries prestige with decent pay. They are forced to take on lower-paying labour-intensive jobs as cleaners or security guards or take higher-paying but difficult or dangerous work such as operating taxis, long-distance trucking, or moving to work in remote areas without their families. This is a harsh and painful reality for many. Some unwilling to accept this reality choose to remain out of the formal workforce or opt to return to their homelands, leaving their families in Canada.

This increased availability of work for women over men often shifts the power balance in many homes where the woman takes on more of the breadwinner role while the husband takes increased domestic duties. When the pressures of making rent payments, paying school fees, managing credit card bills, and satisfying expectant family members in the motherland are added to an already stressful environment, you have the recipe and ingredients for tension to brew. While the objective of a materially better life is accomplished by moving to Canada, there is often an overall decline in the quality of life, particularly in the marriage relationship if these issues are not discussed and managed. Conflict, separation, and divorce are a sad reality in many homes.

The experiences shared here and the interviews with family therapists highlight some of the realities and stresses marriages can go through as a result of the immigration process. They will show how couples can thrive in spite of these pressures and how individuals can keep moving forward, even when the family unit is disrupted and separation and divorce occur.

# Chapter 17:
# Third Time Is the Charm

By B. T., 45-year-old male

I was born in Ghana, West Africa. My father and mother were never married, but they had a good relationship. My mother has passed on but I still communicate with my dad. When I was three years old, I came to Winnipeg, Canada, through my stepfather who has also passed on since. I was too little to remember him. He died somewhere between 1976 and 1979, but he is the one who brought us to Canada. I met my real dad for the first time in 1979 when I went back to Ghana to visit with my mother. He was nice and embracing but I never really saw him after. The next time I saw him, I was probably about nineteen. I didn't know him, but I spent some time with him. It was damaging not growing up with my father. I wish he had been around. I think I would have done much better and made different decisions from sex to school to friendships if I had had him in my life. I was envious of my friends who had two parents. There was a completeness to them. They seemed well put together. In 1987, I was affiliated with an organization

> I was envious of my friends who had two parents. There was a completeness to them.

that connected with the Big Brothers Big Sisters association, which puts together people who need guidance from an older person. I was given a mentor and we were together for a few years. He helped me a lot.

## LOSING MY MOTHER

In 1992, my mother and I went back to Ghana to visit. I was supposed to be returning after two weeks and she was supposed to stay longer, but she never returned. That was her way of tricking me to come back to Canada. She did not plan to come back with me. As a kid, I could never understand why someone would want to stay in Africa. I was now alone and my loneliness really grew. All my friends had families but I didn't. I was alone over holidays and the realization that I was alone grew more and more. I had no siblings or any other relatives around. I would spend my holidays with the family of any girl I would be dating or some close friends' families.

In 2001, my mother died in Ghana, and I wasn't able to go for the funeral. It really dawned on me that it was time for me to settle and get married. My father back in Ghana was urging me to go back and pick a wife from there, and I remember thinking to myself, *That's never going to happen.* There was a lady I met at church. We had broken up but dated a few times previously. We talked it out and decided to get back together. We were both at a place in our lives where we felt it was a good time to settle down.

## GETTING MARRIED

We got married but as soon as we were living together, problems started to surface. We could not consummate the marriage. My wife had a health issue that she claimed not to have been aware of. I later found out that a friend of hers had known about her issue from a long time before. I felt tricked and deceived and angry, and I wanted to confront her and her mother about it but I changed my mind as I thought there would be no point of a confrontation at that point. It was really hurtful. It would have been one thing if she didn't know this condition existed, but now there was evidence that she and her mother knew what they were doing even before I had married her.

## DECIDING TO DIVORCE

The decision to divorce came in three parts. I got up one day and told her we need to leave each other. I told her we were never going to have any children, and it was just going to be an awful marriage. But the next day, I changed my mind. I told her we made a promise to each other and to God that we would be together until death. A number of months later, she came to me and said, "We should stop because this is not fair to you." I should have gotten out at that point, but I said "No, we promised" and our relationship continued.

Some months later, I woke up one day and I just told her "I'm done." I left the house and went for a very long walk. I came home later and we made the decision to end our marriage. It was a hard decision to make because we were still living together, and to make things worse, her brother was living with us as well. Getting him out of the house was difficult. Dividing assets was difficult. I gave her a cheque, and we were done. Living together after deciding to part was very hard. Things were not going the way I had ever envisioned. If I had known things would have turned out this way, I would have never married. She asked if there was a possibility of getting back together and I said "No." She was very bitter and angry from then on. That wasn't what she wanted to hear. I had been under the impression that she was a victim of a health issue, but knowing that she had deceived me made getting back together impossible.

> Knowing that she had deceived me made getting back together impossible.

## COPING WITH CULTURE WARS

Even though we were both Black, marrying into the Caribbean culture is different than marrying into African culture. In African culture, the women leave the man to make decisions for the family, but in Caribbean culture it's "we" make the decisions together. That played out in our marriage. Caribbean women are more independent. We had financial issues. She had a hard time finding work because she did not have the confidence to do well in the interview, so I had to carry the load. Sometimes that was an issue, but it really was the health issue that was the main cause of issues in the marriage. In hindsight, I think I let my emotions drive me. I should have been more patient because the same thing happened to me when I decided to marry again.

## RE-MARRYING AND DIVORCING

I met my second wife at church. I was head over heels for her. I was dating someone else when I met her. My girlfriend at the time showed more humility, but I didn't see her as a future wife. Like me, my second wife had been married before and when we met, we were very happy together. She was terrific— or so I thought. There's a lot of deception in that marriage. She hid so many things, which I only came to discover when we were married. There was a lot of fighting in this relationship. She was a very strong personality. There would be times when I would be yelling and she would be yelling and I would tell myself, *I better get away from her before I hurt her.* There was so much disrespect that in the end I couldn't stay with her. I did not feel loved. I did not want any intimacy with her and definitely didn't want to have kids with her.

## LEARNING TO TRUST

With each divorce I stopped going to church. I felt guilty about divorcing. I was known at church and I was ashamed and embarrassed about being divorced. I went back to the secular life I had before I started

> *felt guilty about divorcing.*

going to church, and my friends in the clubs were doing the exact same stuff after all those years. Most of them hadn't made any progress with their lives. Eventually, I did end up back in church and finding healing. I had to let time pass and do lots of reflection in order to heal and be able to trust women again. I had a lot of anger towards women after the second divorce. Towards the end of my second marriage, I went to Ghana for a trip and I was reminded of the type of women that are in Ghana. I remembered my father's advice years prior, suggesting to go home and get married. I decided to take my dad's earlier advice to come home. He had guided me through my divorces with counsel, wisdom and encouragement. Going back to my roots and upbringing and connecting with that helped me in my third marriage. That process took me about three years.

## REFLECTING ON MARRIAGE

There are a lot of "divorced" people still married. They are together in the same house under the same roof, but they lead different lives. They stay together for the kids or the public but there is no relationship. Sometimes people look cute together in public but when they get home they are not even talking.

My advice to someone considering marriage is know what you are looking for. A lot of deception happens when dating. The person you plan to marry doesn't come out and tell you their issues, so you have to be able to accept that there are things you won't ever know and some things you will come to learn with time. We hide our shame because we are afraid that when the other person really knows us, they will leave us, so understand your needs and your wants but also recognize that you are a highly flawed being. When you start pointing out issues in your partner, remember you are not perfect either. Understand that you are just as flawed as she is. You are just as at fault as she is. Understand how fragile both of you are.

As men, we need to humble ourselves, too. Understand what the woman needs, and learn how to meet those needs. You need to ask yourself what kind of marriage you want. Do you want a good marriage or an exceptional marriage? Do you just want a good-looking woman? Desire an exceptional partner and you will get what you want.

# Chapter 18:
# Unshakable, Unbreakable

By K. P., 42-year-old male

filed for asylum to remain in Canada and did not get it. I appealed the process and that didn't work out either, so I had the option of either voluntarily leaving the country or being deported. Choosing to remain until I was deported meant it would be harder to eventually come back into the country. I opted to leave voluntarily because I had intentions of returning. I was newly married and my wife was in Canada, and I felt Canada was a better place for us than Zimbabwe, my home country. The immigration process was supposed to take a year before I could return, but it ended up taking almost four years.

## BEING A STRANGER IN MY HOMELAND

Being back in Zimbabwe felt like I had gone to a different country than the one I grew up in. I had not been home for twelve years. The buildings were the same, but the people

> Being back in Zimbabwe felt like I had gone to a different country than the one I grew up in.

were different and the culture had changed. The people I had known were not there anymore, and the people I found saw and perceived things differently than I did. Having been away for so long, I didn't realize just how much even I had changed. I was shocked at how poor customer service was. I was shocked at how much worse corruption had gotten. Soon after settling in, I went to apply for an identification card and was in the process of getting my fingerprints taken. The agent had one of my fingerprints done when she said, "It's now my break time." Just like that, she went to take her break, leaving me with my four fingerprints undone. It had taken me a wait from 5:30 a.m. only to get such poor service when my turn finally arrived.

That's just one example of many. I was arrested once because the immigration police did not believe that I was Zimbabwean. They interrogated me, and my dad had to come and get me out of the situation. When I was last in Zimbabwe, it was unheard of to have immigration police walking in the streets.

When I left Zimbabwe for the first time, my original plan was to study medicine and become a doctor, but now I was back after twelve years without any academic qualifications or anything to show for the time I had been away. I did not come with money, cars, or anything to account for my time away. As far as everyone around was concerned, I was just going to be around for a short while. But after people noticed me around and realized I was not going

> I was back after twelve years without any academic qualifications or anything to show for the time I had been away.

anywhere, rumours and questions started spreading about why I was back. Many assumed I had been picked up and kicked out of Canada. I had no opportunity to respond to all the stories being spread, and it was frustrating.

## ACCEPTING MY SITUATION

My parents, being academics, advised me to take a teaching course while figuring out my immigration situation. The course they wanted me to take would take me two years to complete. I debated if I wanted to do a teaching course, but I figured that by the time I'd be finishing the program, my immigration process would have come to its completion. So, I decided against taking the teaching program, despite my parent's insistence. After a year of waiting for immigration, I realized that the process of returning to Canada would take longer than I had originally anticipated. I remember then thinking to myself, *I should have taken dad up on his offer.* I didn't want to be in a situation where people were constantly seeing me around.

I went back to my dad and asked him if the offer was still on the table and, thankfully, it was. After a year of not hearing back from Canadian immigration, it started to make sense for me to do something with myself. My wife was a big part of helping me make the decision to start school. In retrospect, my parents didn't believe I was actually going to return to Canada and thought I was in denial about the whole situation. I, on the other hand, felt that if I budged and went to school, I would be acknowledging that what they were thinking was true. But after thinking it through, I went back to my dad and told him I wanted to do the teaching program but far away from where we lived. In the end, I moved a six-hour drive away from my parents' place for school. Going to school helped me not fixate my mind on the delays with immigration, and it got people who were wondering what I was doing off my back.

## Coping with Frustration

Coping with the whole situation was challenging. My friends were all abroad, and not even my own family members seemed to understand my situation. I mostly kept how I felt to myself. I would talk to my wife and my best friend in the US. Those two were my pillars of strength. We talked and prayed together often. I struggled with my faith and was angry at God for a while. I thought if He really cared, why did things have to end up the way they had? How was what was happening good for my marriage? I went through that phase, but I eventually bounced out of it.

Looking back, leaving my parent's home and doing school was one of the best things I did during that whole process because it allowed me to attend to things quietly without people constantly asking questions. I learned to not talk about the status of my immigration with anybody, and being far from the people who knew me allowed me to do my paperwork without constantly being checked on.

In the end, the timing for me to go to school worked out perfectly. Immigration got back to us and informed us that our application had been successful. This happened a week before the final exam of my teaching course. I had to return to Canada within six months. I went back to my parents and told them I would be leaving the country in two weeks' time. My mom confessed at that time that she had not believed that things would work out for me.

I was back in Canada at the end of December 2015. Within four months of my return to Canada, I took my wife with me back to Zimbabwe for a family reunion. I had a brother in England who I had not seen in a very long time, and he was going home to see my parents, so we thought it would be a great time for all of us to be together

## KEEPING THE FIRE BURNING

Like many African marriages, our marriage went through its challenges with our parents coming around to fully accept our relationship, and that is not the best way to begin a marriage. Me leaving Canada soon after we married made the whole situation more challenging. However, the whole experience of her sticking with me through all that showed me just how great of a woman I had married. She stuck with me during some of the most difficult times of our lives.

> The whole experience of her sticking with me through all that showed me just how great of a woman I had married.

## SHARING LESSONS LEARNED

What I learned out of the whole experience is that God is good, even in His silence. I have learned to be more patient with myself and with others, and I am learning forgiveness for the sake of the people I love. When I went back to Zimbabwe, I remember thinking to myself, *Dreams are overrated. I don't believe in chasing dreams anymore.* I now still believe that dreams can come true, but I also believe that dreams have expiration dates. At least from my experience. If you are going to dream about something, do not procrastinate. I believe that part of living is dreaming. The moment we stop dreaming, we cease to grow and we start dying. The moment you feel you have no purpose to live for, death begins.

# Chapter 19:
# Married But Alone
By P. A., 37-year-old female

My husband and I came to Canada in the fall of 2007. We came to visit my mother-in-law and her husband and were supposed to return after three weeks. But when we saw how Canadians lived, what they had, and the types of lives they led, we decided to stay. My husband already had his Canadian permanent resident status, so it was easy to stay. I called my job and told them I wasn't coming back, and that was it. We had only been married for four months by that time, and only went back to visit home in 2009 when we had our son.

## A NEW BEGINNING

Being in Canada was tough in the beginning. I was homesick and cried a lot. I had never left home before, but I understood it was better for our future to live in Canada. Before moving to Canada, I worked and my life was filled with action, but now I wasn't working and was home most of the time. To add to that, I never spoke English. I was only in my mid-twenties at the time, and I found Canada boring. We lived with my in-laws for a while, and that helped me adjust. When we moved out, I faced several challenges. I was embarrassed to speak to anyone because my English was not very good, so I would stay home all day because I was afraid that someone would speak to me if I left the house. I would only leave the house when my husband was home. I enrolled in English class, and after a while my confidence increased. Then I got my first job. I got pregnant, and having a child changed my life.

## RELATIONSHIP BREAKDOWN

My marriage ended in divorce. I think we both became lazy. It's important to recognize it when your relationship starts to go down. Relationships are hard work. Like many people, we went into our marriage thinking that it would just work but it didn't. After my son was born, I was all about my son, so I completely switched my attention to him and sort of forgot about my husband. It's important to maintain intimacy and sometimes that's forgotten when you start having kids. Kids can take so much attention and it's important to continue to maintain the closeness between man and wife. At some point, we started to fight a lot and we lost respect for each other. It was ugly, and it kept getting worse. I suggested that we go for counselling, but he wasn't interested. He didn't care, and I felt everything fell on me. Every decision, from choosing a school for our son to anything that had to be done for the family, depended on me. We both worked full-time, and he never offered to help with

> completely switched my attention to him and sort of forgot about my husband.

anything in the house. We lost all connection to each other. Once that was gone, it was not easy to get back.

Many people stay in marriages like that and perhaps I, too, could have because I had a child with him. I was young at that time, but I also wanted to be happy. I wanted to see that he cared, but he wasn't bothered, and all we did was fight. He picked up a job where he had to travel, so I was alone with my son quite often, and I had no help from him whatsoever. Our home environment wasn't good for my kid. One day I just went to him and said, "I can't continue; we need to divorce," and all he said was "Okay." He didn't even seem to want to try to fix things. My biggest worry was what was going to happen to my son if we divorced. I wanted to be happy and be loved, and after years of yearning for it and not getting it, divorce became a real option in my mind, but it wasn't an easy decision to make.

My mother was divorced. She divorced for different reasons, so I had experienced it in a different way. My mother was never happy. When she divorced my biological father, it was a terrible situation. He was violent and abusive, so she had to leave. Being a single mother was tough for her. She lived in a time and place, where if you were a single mom people did not have respect for you, so there was pressure to remarry. She got married a second time, and even then, she wasn't happy. Maybe seeing her go through all that put something in me. I'm not sure if that made it easier in my mind to consider getting divorced. By this time, I had a decent job and decent salary, so in my mind I knew that I would be okay even on my own. If the situation was different, perhaps I'd have felt forced to stay, but I knew I could be independent.

## THE STRUGGLE OF DIVORCE

I thought it divorce would be an easy solution to get relief from the whole situation, but it wasn't. For years after, the divorce wasn't an easy thing to get over. The worst part of divorce is dividing assets and sharing custody of our son. We didn't have much, but it was still difficult to agree on how to split our assets. My husband was working and travelling often. In twelve months, he would be gone six or seven months, so we had to figure out how child-support payments could be made fairly as we did not have equal custody for our son. I felt like I was losing while he was gaining. I couldn't work as much as I wanted or even do things like go to the gym. Then there were issues of me learning to trust my husband's parenting when my son was with him, from what food he gave our child to his safety, what entertainment he consumed, and other issues.

> *I thought it divorce would be an easy solution to get relief from the whole situation, but it wasn't.*

I feel bad about it sometimes. I would have wanted my kid to have a normal home. I suffered mild depression. We fought endlessly, and I cried a lot.

## DIVORCE RECOVERY

Having a great support network around me really helped. My brother was around at the time, and he was a real source of strength. It's the simple things that keep one going. I had a choice to make each day whether to be happy or sad. I realized nobody else would make me happy, and I had to enjoy what I still had. Sometimes people set very high expectations and get disappointed when they don't meet those expectations, so I live simply.

I would tell someone considering divorce to really think everything through before the make a decision. Sometimes people are afraid to make that step because they are afraid of being judged and shamed, so they stay in loveless and sometimes abusive marriages. If there is willingness from both parties to save the marriage, the couple should talk and get counselling. Learning how to communicate well is very important, and sometimes counselling can be helpful there. Be specific about how you feel, tell your partner how strongly you feel, how much you are hurting, and what you are thinking. Sometimes one spouse will not realize how serious the situation is. So it's important to communicate things clearly and directly. In the end, each person should come to the decision for themselves. Choosing divorce was the hardest decision I ever had to make.

# Questions and Answers

for Men with Kingsley Moyo,
Marriage Educator, Speaker, and Author

**In North America, roles between men and women are not as rigid as they tend to be in non-Western societies. Men change baby diapers, women can be the breadwinners, and sometimes this causes tension when a couple migrates to this society. How do couples navigate these challenges?**

If I use my African lens to view the Western world, some things will be off. Any person looking at this society through their own paradigm will have difficulty trying to navigate marriage and other relationships. If you had red-coloured glasses and you looked at a white paper, the paper would look red, but someone wearing green-coloured glasses will see the paper as green. There will be conflict and frustration. To navigate this new reality, we have to accept that our context has changed and is governed by different systems. Gender and gender roles are looked at differently. We also need to look at the way we define what culture is. In its simplest sense, culture is a way of coping that a group of people come up with collectively and how they agree they are going to do life.

For example, when I was living in Africa, whenever there was a funeral, everything shut down. We would take food to the house of the mourners and cry for a week or more. Even after, family members still stuck around the mourner's home. It was easily a two-week mourning period, and that's something people in that culture hold and accept about how they mourn. In North America, you might get flowers or have people text you their condolences, so when you use your non-Western lens to look at that, you might feel that the people here are insensitive or uncaring. When we talk about roles mixing, we are usually trying to transport an African cultural context and bring it into the North American cultural context. So I'd say to remove those glasses and start asking questions: what are you experiencing, why are things done differently? Ask questions and embrace your new reality.

**Men seem to have it harder adjusting to this environment. In some cases, men have even left their families in order to go back home to jobs where they had more status. What's your advice to men on how they can continue to find that sense of purpose, despite the challenges that come with the immigration experience?**

Dr. Miles Munroe often used to say, "If the purpose of a thing is unknown, abuse is inevitable." We sometimes find that happens with men a lot. A man who might have been a doctor or manager overseeing a lot of people will oftentimes want to be in that same position when he moves abroad. We need to ask ourselves what the purpose of our jobs is. If your purpose is to provide for your family, then even if you end up a taxi driver, you will be content. It is important to consider the reason behind why someone might feel that sense of loss when they migrate.

Awareness of what a person is experiencing is important. Men in the diaspora pass through various stages and for different lengths of time. I will call them these stages: awe, frustration, adjustment, and acceptance. The phases almost mimic the stages that someone would go through when grieving, as explained below.

## AWE

This is the first stage when a man comes to the diaspora. This is the time of excitement—big buildings, opportunity, and fascination. This is the period before the dust settles down and the reality hasn't yet hit. This is a period when you call back home every day to tell people you've made it and that your family is doing well. This is before the kids have started to rebel, before their accents have changed, and before they have the nerve to talk back, and the man is still in charge of his domain.

## FRUSTRATION

Then there is the frustration stage. This is when you begin to see barriers. You see prejudice, you realize that there are language barriers, that the sort of work you desire is not easily attainable. These things can make a marriage or the relationship with kids difficult. Your wife may have found work and now is the breadwinner while you remain home to cook, which is almost unheard of in an African cultural context. It hurts many men's egos to be in that position.

In the frustration stage, you realize that things are not working and you begin to see emotional changes like anger become more present in your life. You see physical changes. The food is different and you are less active because of the winter and other things. Then there are psychological changes, like depression, which many men don't know how to recognize or associate with being weak. The people that typically go back home are the people that don't move from the frustration stage, because everything is just not working out. Those that make it out of this stage are those that become aware and look at their worldviews and go into the third phase.

## ADJUSTMENT

The adjustment phase happens when you have learned how to navigate the system. You know who to talk to get a job, you know what medical tests are out there, how to get further education, and you have learned to find meaning in worship and connecting with people from your community. You accept that you are raising Western kids and that women adjust differently to this culture.

## ACCEPTANCE

This is the last phase. This is when you look back and realize it has been twenty years since you moved to Canada, your kids are in university, grandkids are on the way, and you are comfortable with being a taxi driver.

**In many African households, the man is considered the head of the family– an idea that is not as readily accepted in sections of Western society. Men also have to grapple with the fact that women are much more empowered in the West, and men sometimes feel that they receive the short end of the stick when they migrate. How can men**

**adjust to these new realities and remain agents of stability and security for their families?**

Someone might be reading this and thinking that the idea of man as the head of the home as being almost nonsensical. However, it is a very real issue in many immigrant communities, and it is not some small thing that doesn't affect marriage relationships. One thing I pay attention to is how these words are used by individuals from different cultural contexts. I've listened to immigrants speaking sometimes what people are saying is what you would call literal translation. For example, there is a saying in my culture that if you translate it literally says, "You cannot kill a snake with a long fire," but there is no such thing as a long fire. The meaning of that saying is that a big problem does not require a big solution.

Sometimes the way people speak and how it might be understood can mean very different things. We have to look at what "being the head of the home" means in our cultural context. I tend to believe the head of the home doesn't mean the same thing for every family. In the African context, we understand that women are not less than men. They have their value and their place. But someone who looks into that culture with their own lens may say, "Women are ill-treated." Another thing to consider is that culture and values are not synonymous. Culture informs our values. Culture is dynamic, but values do not change. Sometimes we immigrants experience trouble in this context because we approach things with a rigid cultural perspective that we are not willing to change.

As a kid, one of the rules my parents had was that we got home before sundown. But that rule would not make sense for me to impose on to my Canadian-raised children when sundown here can be as early as 4 p.m. My kids will wonder what's wrong with me. So that's really something we have to pay attention to, so that our homes and marriages are not affected. You can still be the head of your household or have authority the way you want it, but make sure it's a communal agreement. If it works in your home and everyone is okay with it, then that's fine.

I have so much respect for Muslim women who wear a hijab. I don't fully understand it, but I had to pause when I heard one woman say, "I don't know what your problem is, but I am fine with it." That made me realize, "I am not Muslim. I am not from that culture, so what right do I have to go and tell them how to dress? Sometimes, it is not so much that men have lost their status when they come here, but that what was valued in their home countries is no longer valued in Western society. Where I come from, it would be unheard of to call someone older than you by their first name. Here, that doesn't matter. We should be open to adjusting our culture but maintaining our values.

> We should be open to adjusting our culture but maintaining our values.

**How can couples manage conflict before it ends in divorce?**

Often, what I see among immigrants is that people tend to wait up until things are very bad before they seek help, and when they seek help, they hope that the counsellor will come up with a miracle to save their relationship. I want to emphasize that couples need to get help early. In many cultures, it is not that counselling doesn't happen. It's just that counselling has taken on a different form here. In other places, it's family members who sit a couple down to resolve conflict, but that often isn't possible here. In any conflict, both people contribute to the conflict. Both parties are responsible for apologizing. We tend to weigh our pain and anger and say, "Since you wronged me more, you need to apologize first." We wait until the other person comes to apologize, which doesn't always happen. But if we approach conflict from the perspective that both people contributed to the conflict, we need to be able to own up to that. And once we do, then healing can begin.

Sometimes immigrants don't trust therapists and counsellors for various reasons like cultural differences or language barriers. But these trained professionals can be of great help. There are also other resources that couples can use; online courses which allow you to learn about each other from the comfort of your home. There are communities like churches, men's groups, and other groups which can help people be raw and honest with each other.

People tend to make only first-order changes in their relationships. First-order changes are small changes—changes that just tinker with the system. For example, if your phone is not working, turning it off and on is a first-order change. But if you take the phone to someone who fixes phones and get the device pulled apart and have things replaced, that's a lasting change. As couples, when there is a fight about parenting or the dishes or sexual discordance in the marriage, by just making first-order changes, nothing changes.

We need to make those lasting changes, otherwise the same cycle just keeps repeating and eventually the couple becomes numb to the conflict and drifts apart. The conversation that happens after the conflict is the most crucial conversation. In the heat of the conversation you are stonewalling, defending, and fighting, but after the conflict when you are thinking straight is when you can admit fault and guilt and talk about how you can make those second-order changes, which are lasting changes. People tend to wait until conflict happens, but you can do preventative work, like going to seminars that teach about anger and conflict, listening to podcasts, reading books, or being around people who want to grow.

**When a couple decides to divorce, what are some of the things they should people think about?**

By the time a couple divorces, they have already gone through a lot of problems, arguments, and conflict, and that creates a lot of emotional scars and trauma. The trauma is sometimes underestimated, because we often think about the physical aspects of trauma only. However, there is emotional and psychological trauma and that affects the way you function, your productivity, and your health due to the stress being experienced. There is a lot more to divorce than just thinking, "I will get a divorce and everything will be okay." There are psychological effects, depression, and anxiety—you may never trust and love the same way again. It affects the next generation, because children watch everything going on, their moods get affected, they disconnect from their schoolwork and relationships with other people, and it affects their own relationships as adults later in life.

There are physiological effects as well. Stress is one of the biggest contributors of health problems in the US[4]. Cancer, flu, and high-blood pressure sometimes get accelerated when a person is under extreme stress. That said, every divorce is different. I have a firm conviction that for any people that want a relationship to work, it will work. For any couple where both people say, "I want it to work" and genuinely mean it, I can say that in ninety-nine per cent of cases, the relationship will work. It means they are ready to understand, to change, empathize, grow, and forgive. Some people have gone through infidelity or abuse, while others are fleeing for their lives, but I am not referring to those cases. I am referring to what are usually classified as irreconcilable differences. Weigh everything when the step to divorce is being considered. It's not just about finances, as many people often mistakenly assume.

> For any people that want a relationship to work, it will work.

**What practical ideas can you suggest for couples to "keep the fire burning?"**

We want to move relationships beyond functional to excellent or exceptional. While it might seem like things like romance and vacation are not emphasized in non-Western cultures, life

---

4 "Stress A Major Health Problem in the U.S., Warns APA." https://www.apa.org/news/press/releases/2007/10/stress. Accessed 5 Apr. 2021.

in many of those places is not as busy as it is here. Life starts at sunlight and slows down at sundown. In North America, people work odd hours, weekends, and public holidays. But in many non-Western contexts, that isn't how life functions, so the need for time to relax and do those sorts of activities is not as critical there as it is here. Those societies also have their ways of coping within their contexts. City people go to the village to rest and, as mentioned already, there is more relaxing time built into each day. Many non-Western cultures are more collectivist, so people are around friends and family every day and recharge that way. Those things are built into the culture. In North America, things tend to be more individualistic. You may see friends once a week, because life is so busy with work and other things.

Romance is crucial. It's about looking for excitement in the marriage. Couples need to do random things and do spontaneous activities together. When someone buys a car, they clean it, take it for oil changes, and service it, but people get married and don't maintain the relationship and think the relationship will just keep running without any work.

When a couple first gets married, they are excited, and it doesn't take long before long they start to really discover each other. The dates reduce, time spent together reduces, and the couple stops growing together. Couples that grow together experience greater intimacy, so find out what you like and grow and pursue things together. Play games, have fun, pursue shared goals, and look to grow in all spheres of life: socially, academically, spiritually, emotionally. Do what you did when you were dating.

**What advice would you give to a man who feels, "Nothing I ever do makes her happy"?**

Oftentimes, when you hear someone say that "Whatever I do is not acceptable," it's often an indicator that there are problems in other areas of the relationship that haven't been addressed. The issue may seem to be the way one does dishes, but no matter how those dishes are done, as long as that other issue is left unaddressed, there will always be trouble in the relationship. The way you show up in one area of your life is the way you show up in all areas. So if you have an issue in one area of the relationship, all areas are affected.

Also, in many cases like that, there are no clear boundaries in the relationship. Boundaries are not a negative thing. Boundaries create connection. If a woman says, "I need help with the dishes" and the dishes are the man's responsibility, that lady should let the man have that responsibility and own it. If the dishes are not done the way you like as a woman, just leave it. You have given him that responsibility, and he will eventually figure it out. More often than not, the job won't be done the way the partner wants and ends up nagging that the job wasn't done properly. Even if it's not done to perfection, let him do it. If a woman says to you as a man, "This is what I want you to do," do it. And if you are a woman, you need to learn to let go and let the man do what he said he'd do. Boundaries need to be clear.

# Questions and Answers

for Women with Margaret Tuimising,
Marriage and Family Therapist (MFT)

**When couples move to Canada, they sometimes start to experience challenges in their marriages they didn't have before. What is it about the immigration experience that causes many of these issues to suddenly surface?**

Change brings stress to relationships. People many times are dealing with a sense of loss from the things and relationships they left behind and that affects the marriage relationship. The partners are making sudden adjustments to their ways of life; some are struggling with language adjustments, changing roles, changing behaviours in their kids, and all that can be confusing and add to the stress the couple is experiencing.

**Sometimes the challenge for women is that they continue to do everything they did back home but now take on additional roles here. For example, they might have been the ones doing all the housework and looking after kids, but when they migrate, they feel or are expected to do all that plus the additional roles that come with being**

**a full-time worker. What can women do to avoid getting burned out?**

Firstly, women need to be aware that they can't do it all and need to embrace and practice self-care. In the places we come from, it's usually easy to get help even if the husband doesn't help out with domestic duties. Women need to come to terms with the fact that that is not the reality in Canada. They should not feel guilty about asking their husbands and family members to help them with chores.

Secondly, trust. Sometimes women do so much because they don't trust that their spouses or family members can do things as well as they can, so women need to be flexible with their standards, let go, and trust other people to do things believing that it will be okay in the end.

Thirdly, women should communicate their needs. Sometimes men can't hear what is not said, so it's okay to ask for help.

**You talked about self-care. For many who never grew up around such ideas and were brought up in an environment that says women have to look out for others, it can be difficult to embrace ideas of self-care, which seem selfish.**

Many women raised in non-Western countries grow up being taught only to be there for other people, but that's something we need to adjust because that is hard to sustain in this environment. In non-Western environments, women have their own ways of taking care of themselves. It might be them going to the market or to the river to chat with friends, but in this environment, people are constantly on the go, so it's important to consciously seek out time for yourself. Women need to keep in mind that they cannot take care of others if they are not healthy. It's not selfish to take care of yourself.

**What self-care suggestions do you have for immigrant women?**

I'd suggest that women develop some hobbies. For some, I know the idea of hobbies is a foreign concept, but it's important to do something that you like for yourself. It could be simple things like walking in the park, music, exercise, whatever. Find like-minded people with who you can go out for tea, watch a movie, or exercise, and develop a community of friends. It is very important that you have people and activities that pull you out of your regular routine.

**It seems women have an easier time adjusting than men when they migrate. What advice would you have for men to help them with the challenges of adjusting to a new culture?**

I would suggest the following:

1. Men and women need to come to accept their new reality. Many come here and spend all their time thinking of what used to be, regretting, and being bitter and angry. Doing that doesn't help you enjoy the here and now. Being able to accept and let go of what was and accepting what is, is an important part of the process.

2. Men can learn to find meaning in new things. Find things that you like, and things you can develop. That builds

confidence and makes one happier and that makes things easier. If being the head of the home and making the most money gave you satisfaction and you can't play that role anymore, find something that gives your life new meaning. Getting into groups of newcomers and finding people going through the same thing you are going through really helps. Men can get together with other men going through the same challenges and can laugh and share experiences and ideas while making friends.

3. Be open. If you chose to just live in the past, it just makes settling in that much harder. Try out new things, and you will slowly start to enjoy new things that you never thought you would.

**There are women out there who feel stuck and maybe are even considering divorce. Are there things you can recommend for women who might feel "stuck" in their situations?**

Sometimes things just don't work out, and relationships end. Women should first figure out whether or not the situation can be salvaged. Sometimes there's so much pain and anger that a separation for a while can be helpful. Ending a relationship is one of the most difficult decisions a person can make. In many cases, people want things to work and can make them work. One has to have the courage to accept that they are facing a challenge and ask for help when things are not going well. If a person decides to make the decision to separate or divorce her partner, she needs to ask herself what that will mean for her and the children.

**When people decide to divorce, it can be quite difficult, especially for women who, in most cases, have primary custody of the kids. How does someone move on from the shame they might feel after a divorce?**

Life after divorce is a whole new reality. People need to access whatever supports are available from community groups to therapy. Sometimes it may mean changing associations and being around people and places where you feel supported and understood. Detach yourself from associations that judge you and label you. Also, people who are divorced need to remember that a failed relationship is not a failed life. It's never just one person's fault that the relationship failed.

**What are some things you would suggest to couples to strengthen their relationships?**

*People who are divorced need to remember that a failed relationship is not a failed life.*

Most things are suggestions that people already know but tend to forget. While life here can be busy, we need to remember to ascribe importance to our relationships. Couples need to seek out time to build their marriages. Many people think their work is done when they put a ring on their partner and sometimes feel that as long as they are working and bringing money that their work is done, but in reality, that's when the work begins. People need to spend time connecting with each other. They need to remember some of the things they did when they first met and do them over. Buy her flowers, call her in the middle of the day—people need to keep doing those things. Couples should also learn to do things together socially and spiritually and create memories. It's also important to know and actively practice each other's love language.

# Acknowledgements

I would like to thank all the individuals and professionals who allowed their stories and expertise to be used for this project. These individuals gave their knowledge and time and cared enough to allow me to use their stories and share their expertise so that others can be helped. To all of you, I sincerely appreciate you and your trust in me and this project.

I also want to thank my wife who has been my number one cheerleader and for allowing me the freedom to spend countless hours writing and interviewing. I thank my siblings and my parents for always believing in me and for laying the foundation through which I see and understand the world. I thank God, too, for life and planting in me the passion and determination to accomplish this work.

CPSIA information can be obtained
at www.ICGtesting.com
Printed in the USA
LVHW091753210322
713801LV00030B/64

9 781039 118454